W9-CAM-982

vintage fashion

VINTAGE FASHION: COLLECTING AND WEARING
VINTAGE CLASSICS, 1900–1990
Copyright © 2006 by CARLTON BOOKS

All rights reserved. No part of this book may be used or
reproduced in any manner whatsoever without written
permission except in the case of brief quotations embodied in
critical articles and reviews. For information, address Collins
Design, 10 East 53rd Street, New York, NY 10022.

HarperCollins books may be purchased for educational, business,
or sales promotional use. For information, please write: Special
Markets Department, HarperCollins Publishers, 10 East 53rd
Street, New York, NY 10022.

First Edition

First published in the United States and Canada in 2007 by:
Collins Design
An Imprint of HarperCollins*Publishers*
10 East 53rd Street
New York, NY 10022
Tel: (212) 207-7000
Fax: (212) 207-7654
collinsdesign@harpercollins.com
www.harpercollins.com

Distributed throughout the United States and Canada by:
HarperCollinsPublishers
10 East 53rd Street
New York, NY 10022
Fax: (212) 207-7654

Executive Editor: Lisa Dyer
Senior Art Editor: Emma Wicks
Designer: Adam Wright
Copy Editors: Nicky Gyopari, Diana Craig, and Libby Willis
Picture Researchers: Paul Langan and Jenny Lord
Production: Caroline Alberti
Special Photography: Emma Wicks

Library of Congress Control Number: 2007923538

ISBN: 978-0-06-125201-3
ISBN-10: 0-06-125201-8

First Printing, 2007
Printed and bound in Dubai

COLLINS|DESIGN
An Imprint of HarperCollins*Publishers*

vintage fashion

collecting and wearing designer classics

foreword by
Zandra Rhodes

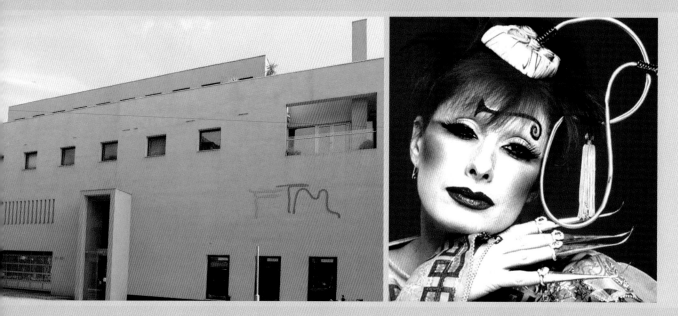

Foreword

Vintage – what wonders this word now conjures up when linked with fashion! A magical harvest of wearable art! A wine from a past season that must be dipped into, sampled, and tasted; old, yes, but the garment is a survivor of the twentieth century and as such has become a classic of importance.

The world is just realizing that fashion (meaning the clothes and the fabrics they are made from) has been lifted from the status of what we just wear to being an art form. It is the most recent of the acknowledged art forms. Toward the second half of the twentieth century, designers were acknowledged and were no longer hidden in the background behind the manufacturer's label. Even more recently, textile designers and their contribution to the final garment have started to be recognized.

I founded the Fashion and Textile Museum in Bermondsey, London, to ensure that British designers would be remembered and because textile designers must be memorialized for their contribution. Seeing so many of these vintage examples creates an awareness and hope that these will now be preserved for posterity, perhaps magically framed and carefully displayed.

The vintage clothes pictured in this book must have had adventures, and they have survived ill treatment and the toll of years. They have passed through the time warp of being considered outmoded and, God forgive, old-fashioned, and have come through with flying colors into the twenty-first century. These vintage clothes represent what is best, and show the distinctive characteristics of each designer. Exactly like vintage wine, they represent what is outstanding and special about their particular period. Here within this book, so many of the key looks of the fast-moving twentieth century have been painstakingly hunted down and researched, with photographs from the relevant decade; or the clothes themselves have been photographed, captured in print like gorgeous pressed flowers, indicating just what richness these garments and their designers have given the world.

Suddenly here is a book laying vintage out clearly and chronologically. The genius of Dior and his New Look; the flowering of the Swinging '60s in London, side by side with the Parisian movement of Courrèges; the surrealistic approach started by Schiaparelli but continued later in the century by designers such as Moschino; vandalism, or unusual treatment of fabrics, or even raw edges, have entered the design vocabulary, while incredible pleating techniques tentatively started by Fortuny have been pioneered and taken to new heights by Issey Miyake and his school. This book clearly shows periods without print, where sculptural, unsolvable, incredible shapes have been made with fabric twisting around the body, sometimes figure-hugging, sometimes not (how did the designer ever come up with that?). So too can be seen the early Chanel, who used woven cloth and contained her garment edges with woven braid borders or ribbons, a look of such strength and simplicity that its seeds have endured and grown into a whole empire worldwide.

*Colors, shapes, patterns, and plains;
so much is to be found in these pages.
When was everything plain and
subdued? When were printed patterns
to the fore? When were printed
patterns overwhelming? When were
they used as a totally integral part of
the garment where it could not have
been that shape were it not for
the print?* Zandra Rhodes

'20s '30s '40s '50s

Introduction

A historical record, a cherished possession, a personal belonging that may be described as a "second skin": Favorite items of clothing have the power to transform the body and spirit of women the world over and always have. The interest in vintage clothing ties deeply into this almost physical response to fashion. Vintage pieces not only capture a historical moment in time but in themselves can be works of absolute and unique beauty. The techniques and handworking of previous decades, before mass production, can be seen on pieces up to the early 1900s in the United States and later in Europe. After this, factories had learned to mass-produce clothes and a vast number of off-the-rack styles became available to the public. Gone were the days when a handful of couturiers set the pace for style and local seamstresses copied

patterns from Paris or fashion magazines. With the reliance upon manufacturers who produced the clothes, there was some loss of individuality. However, vintage pieces reclaim this by transcending the limitations of what's stylish or available today – a 1930s bias-cut Vionnet gown or a 1950s Christian Dior dress can be stand-out stunning anytime. Why choose from the ready-to-wear options produced for you when the whole history of fashion is available?

Several trends set in earlier decades have developed into classics: The shift dress, the twinset, the tailored suit, the bias-cut gown, the little black dress, and many more have not drastically changed since their inception. Even today couture designers plunder the back catalogs in order to study, copy, and learn from the masters of years before, often mimicking details, such as pin tucks or seamfinishing,

'60s '70s '80s

as well as prints, the cut of a pattern, or surface decoration, such as beading, lacework, or ribbonwork, in their own designs.

In this book vintage pieces are charted through a framework of fashion history over 90 years of the last century, celebrating the most significant designers, developments, and movements of each decade, which have contributed to fashion as we know it. Starting from the time when Parisian haute couture houses led the way, at the onset of the twentieth century, four writers chronicle the arrival of the flapper, the austerity fashions of the war years, Christian Dior's New Look, the Swinging '60s, punk and antifashion movements, the new romanticism, and the power-suited 1980s — all in examples of collectible vintage samples from the time. Giving an overview of changing trends, the book invests the reader with the knowledge necessary to identify pieces as belonging to specific time periods, to distinguish between various fashion movements, and to understand how and why certain fashions were worn at the time.

In many ways today's fashions evolve from the needs and desires of women, rather than the social diktats, conventions, and mores that once set the tone of the day. Although fashion has been liberated from the constraints of society and tradition, at this particular vantage point in the twenty-first century, we can look back, learn, and reinvent, taking what we like from fashions that have gone before, wearing clothing in different ways from those originally intended, or simply collecting favorite pieces for the sheer unadulterated pleasure of owning something incomparably beautiful, rare, and elusive.

1900-29

At the turn of the century, the sun shone for a privileged few. Fashion was dictated from the top, and the decorative female in her frills and flounces seemed to waft through society while caged in an ironclad corset. As modernism gathered pace, both the corset and the suffocating Victorian values of the time were torn apart, and in 1909 a new, linear silhouette came into fashion. Societal norms were challenged, and an explosion of originality and progressive ideas in art, film, psychology, and the role of women took place.

Ethnic elements, oriental themes, ancient Greece, and Japanese prints all influenced fashion, shown in exotic-styled motifs, the natural form, and the curvilinear designs of the avant-garde. Added to this, following the tragedy of the First World War and the arrival of post-1918 fashion, women went wild. Hemlines went up, waistlines went down, and flappers danced the Charleston, the bunny hug, and to the new, hot sound of jazz. Fringe, beads, and tassels ornamented short dresses worn above the knee, and the accent was on youth and "misbehaving."

By the 1920s the media age was beginning. People acquired their sartorial ideas not from their "betters" but from listening to the radio, copying stars in the movies, and reading about the fashions in *Vogue* and *Vanity Fair*. The growing popularity of sports such as tennis and cycling prompted a new and simpler look. Jean Patou, Madeleine Vionnet, and Coco Chanel were among the designers who created the first modern style for women, still seen today.

The New Century

The last decade of the nineteenth century – also called the belle époque – and the first 14 years of the twentieth century, up to the First World War, were a time of untrammeled gaiety and luxury. The later years are often called the Edwardian period, after Britain's King Edward VII (reigned 1901–10), whose hedonistic lifestyle set the tone for this period. Edwardian fashions were status symbols, and, due to the restrictive silhouette, had an erotic element as well. The constricting dress and the exuberance of frills and flounces were testimony to the leisured life of the wearer. The Edwardian silhouette, with its tiny waist, could not have been created without the corset. Straight-fronted, it pushed the pelvis back and the bosom forward, achieving the fashionable S-shape, balanced by a protruding hipline that was svelte and padded. Prominent but low, the bust seemed to overhang and was then festooned with various laces, ruffles, and ribbons. The skirt fitted very tightly over the hips, so there was no room for pockets (small bags came into fashion), then fanned out toward the floor.

Corsets were made of whalebone and encased the wearer in ironclad dignity. They were then covered in satin, brocade, silk, or *coutil* (a closely woven canvas). Trimmed with lace and small roses, they could be bought in black for evening or the pretty palettes of pale blue, pinks, and mauves. Garters were attached to the corset or worn on a separate belt, and even these were covered in ribbons and had gilt clasps.

By the 1900s the froufrou sound of lace petticoats was enough to stir the minds of ardent men. Patterned machine laces, in particular Valenciennes and Chantilly (black), were most popular of all and eagerly bought by those who could not afford the real thing.

Net dresses were fashionable (machine-made bobbin net was easy to make) and often worn with a silk underdress. Embroidered on this plain net "canvas" were chenille floral motifs: Roses, lilies, and other flowers appeared on necklines, sleeves, and bodices. Bunches of lace (jabots) attached to the front of bodices, and gilt braid and seams bound with silk satin, rounded off this pretty look. Intricate lacework with floral patterns, pin tucks, and insertions created contrasting texture on lawn fabric. All fulfilled the

PAGE 10 Black peplum-bodiced velvet dress, trimmed with bands of velvet, with a white batiste turnover collar, by Paul Poiret, 1924. A fine example of modernism in fashion, it is worn by model Dinarzade (Petra Clive).

Edwardian love of fussy detail and were dominant characteristics of the period.

The all-important blouse

Figuring largely in ladies' sartorial repertoire, the blouse varied from the severely tailored masculine style, with detachable starched collars and cuffs complete with tie, to highly elaborate confections. The tailored blouse was immortalized by the Gibson Girl (created by American illustrator Charles Dana Gibson), whose casual elegance and independent spirit – exemplified by her love of sports – made her a model for young American women.

Romantic-style, hand-embroidered lace blouses were back-buttoned and usually white. They had finely tucked bodices and tucked sleeves. Often edged with white embroidery or machine-made lace, they were made from flimsy muslin, Japanese silk, and zephyr, and conveyed a fragile femininity. Three-quarter-length sleeves were in the fashionable Magyar style – tight-fitting with undersleeves that matched the neckline, puffed at the shoulders and laced at the cuff.

The Edwardian neck was often tightly enclosed in a high collarette of boned chiffon and lace, giving the wearer a regal bearing. Catalogs featured both the V-neck and the round neck, worn with little modesty squares in the neckline. Over the blouse a woman might wear a bolero *visite*, generally of chiffon and lace.

Dresses and tea gowns

Store catalogs of the era featured afternoon frocks made out of muslin with white cotton foundation bodices fastened with hooks at the front and frilled with machine-made Valenciennes lace. Embroidered motifs, flowers, and piping were also popular. Tucked gathers at the neckline gave a square, ruched-yoke effect.

SIGNATURE EDWARDIAN ELEMENTS:

- Long trailing skirts that fitted tightly over the hips, flowed to the knees, then fanned out
- High necks enclosed in stiff lace
- Wide puffed sleeves with close-fitting undersleeves
- Bodices fully boned to the neckline
- Ruffles and spangles as allover decoration on dresses
- Pin tucks as detailing, and used in blouses and dresses
- Low-cut necklines and bare backs for eveningwear
- Machine net used as a fabric in its own right, from which whole dresses were made

LEFT With layers of lace for structure, a high, slimline collar forced the neck to be held erect, contributing to the long, curved torso line and a well-bred manner. Collars were shaped to reach as high as possible at the back of the jaw, behind the ear, and this uneven shaping is characteristic of the era, persisting throughout the first decade of the century until the First World War.

LEFT The deep V construct of the lace bodice accentuates the low bustline. The delicate rose color of the dress is also a period detail, as the palette was generally subdued and shades had names such as "ashes of rose."

LEFT Three-quarter-length Magyar lace sleeves are overlaid by the ornately embroidered bodice sleeves.

OPPOSITE Edwardian vintage lace dress, by G. E. Spitzer, Vienna, circa 1905. Worn with a straight-fronted corset that molded the torso into an S-bend, the dress created a silhouette of a full bottom, narrow waist, and low single bustline. The straighter skirt replaced the full Victorian skirt.

LEFT Turn-of-the-century fashion: Deep, low bodices, decorated with flowers, lace, and embroidery, bestow the all-important Edwardian S-bend silhouette.

The deification of all that is feminine was embodied in the Edwardian evening dress. Floating dresses of sheer net, a froth of chiffon and soft faille, with bands of pleated silk draped over the shoulder and crossed at the waist, came in sweet pea and Jordan almond delicacies of tone. A rounded décolletage was scooped low off the shoulders and filled in with a modest ruffle of white chiffon. This would be festooned with more ruffles, tulle, lacings, and glass beads forming sprays of leaves, flowers, and ribbons.

By this time tea gowns were usually very elaborate confections of silk or wool and lavish lace trimmings. Worn to entertain visitors for tea, they featured the modest high neck. Often draped or pleated, they had deep gathered flounces and lace-edged ruffles.

The tailor-made costume

Appealing to the independent woman, tailored suits became a kind of uniform for the enlightened. The skirt, made of tweed, serge, or linen, was high-waisted, shorter than before, and trimmed with braid and buttons. Worn with the starched blouse (see page 13), the suit was completed by a smart tailored jacket, often of silk, serge, or wool, and lined with solid-colored fabric or appliqué. Often worn with a vest, this severe jacket style sometimes featured leather cuffs and collar.

ABOVE AND LEFT A lady's jacket, circa 1905, is ornately decorated with military-style frogging and embroidered epaulettes. The back view, above, is richly detailed, with a black yoke reminiscent of a military uniform.

1912   1913   1913

The First Couture Houses

By the turn of the century, "gay Paree" was the epicenter of fashion and became a regular stop for the leisured classes and royals visiting the new couture houses of Doucet, Paquin, Callot Soeurs, Poiret, Lucile, and Redfern. Earlier, Charles Worth had elevated the status of the dressmaker to that of an artist. In his luxurious showrooms at 7 rue de la Paix, Paris – the first couture house to open – his creations were snapped up.

Charles Worth's lavish evening and reception gowns were almost as important as the events to which they were worn. His ingenuity in combining different fabrics and his creation of the backswept bustle skirt allowed a unique fall of fabric, while his singular cut and sense of ornament were his hallmarks. He sometimes used fabric with large floral motifs, specially woven so as to follow the figure.

By 1908 Paul Poiret had revolutionized the silhouette, and the overornamented Edwardian silhouette gave way to a high-waisted empire-line dress. A "natural" style inspired by the art deco and fauve movements, with their bold colors and surface decoration, came in. Poiret's Hellenic dresses were designed in the manner of classical Greek drapery to reveal the natural contours of the body; hanging from the shoulders, they would drape around the female form. Materials with fluid qualities, such as muslin, light silk, satin, and tulle, were used to create the draped effect. Poiret's gowns were simple and either in solid colors or with geometric designs. His revolutionary *jupe culotte* (harem skirt) and kimonos were just as outré.

Color and artistry, beautifully draped dresses, evening wraps, opulent furs, and extravagant outerwear are all hallmarks of the house of Paquin, founded by Jeanne Beckers, who became known as Jeanne Paquin, and Isidore Jacobs. In materials such as muslin and voile, Paquin created exciting visual effects with light and texture. Beads and sequins, shirring and ruching, dotted net ribbon trim and padded appliqué were used to create a heightened visual quality, and she loved to combine unconventional materials, such as fur on a light pastel gown or chiffon with serge.

Other designers were clothing the new rich clients. Callot Soeurs favored individuality and had a superb understanding of old velvet and lace, which it used for elaborate day dresses, and of heavy satin, for evening. Jacques Doucet, meanwhile, was known for his excellent workmanship and quality, and the British house of Redfern developed tailored yachting suits, riding habits, dresses, shawls, and mantles for the upper classes.

OPPOSITE Illustration of dresses by Jacques Doucet, Lucile (Lucy Kennedy, later Lady Duff Gordon), and Charles Worth, dated 1912, 1913, and 1913, respectively.

LEFT, BELOW, AND BELOW LEFT Black 1920s Paquin dress with pink embroidery. Paquin's signature color was pink, but she was also known for her dramatic use of black. Deep slits on the bodice and the back sleeves, a handkerchief hem, and vertical ruching at the waist are some of the unique details on this rare piece. There would have been a ribbon threaded through on the back.

Early Innovations and Influences

ABOVE Sonia Delaunay's "simultaneous" color contrasts on a painted surface. Artist, printmaker, and fashion designer, Delaunay was a leader of the Orphism movement, an attempt to soften cubism with lyrical color.

As fashion and the female body freed themselves from the constraints of the stranglehold, daring new techniques sprang up. The avant-garde artists used bright geometric shapes printed directly onto the textile, creating a form of moving painting. New ways of wrapping the body were created – the ancient craft of pleating was resurrected, and techniques such as cutting the dress along the bias produced new elastic drapes that molded, rather than bifurcated, the female body.

Color and textile design
In the years before the First World War, new elements outside fashion influenced trends in a big way. The painter Sonia Delaunay covered fashion fabrics with patterns of colors in contrasting gradations – deep blue, black, white, yellow, or green, or softer combinations of different browns and beiges. Her "simultaneous"

dresses, with their geometric blocks of bright color, had an energy about them and were a kind of antifashion. Delaunay's embroidered coats (executed in *point du jour* using wool, cotton, and silk); her *robes poèmes* (poem dresses), featuring lines of poetry beside swatches of bright colors; and her brightly embroidered beachwear were all dynamic visions of modernity.

An inventor of revolutionary fabrics, Mariano Fortuny devised vertical pleating, a process that he patented in 1909, whereby silk and cotton had an elastic quality and flowed over the contours of the female form. Pleats, often in the new "painterly" colors, such as Nile green, blues, and soft reds, were twisted like skeins of yarn. He overpainted and dip-dyed again and again to achieve the desired shade. Silk cording was laced with heavy beads, then hand-stitched along hems, seams, and neckline to give weight to the dress. Fortuny combined his color effects with stenciling, producing striking effects on heavy brocades and velvets, and incorporated textile patterns from East Asia and the Islamic world.

Bias cutting

With the bias cut, Madame Vionnet rethought the relationship between fabric and flesh. She cut the fabric diagonally across the grain to produce a Grecianesque drape, which seemed to spiral around the body. Reduced to their most basic lines, her dresses – often in silk, such as crepe de chine – were not so much fitted but fell in vertical folds that seemed to move with the body. With their clever simplicity and ease of movement, Vionnet's body-hugging dresses were of the modern age. They had no fastenings and required minimal underwear. She was also famous for her handkerchief points and the blouson dress, which was tied around the hips in a front bow.

Orientalism

During the 1910s, fashion looked to non-Western cultures. A craze for all things oriental was seen in the proliferation of Japanese prints and kimono-style dresses. Oriental embroideries and exotic colors, such as dark green, antique gold, and rich reds, were juxtaposed with traditional pastels to create a new, vibrant look. With Sergei Diaghilev's 1909 Ballets Russes and Poiret's 1912 Minaret collection, Eastern-influenced fashions swept in.

The Chanel suit

Radical in its understatement, the Chanel suit in jersey is more a way of life than an article of clothing. Chanel pared away fussy details and adapted male garments to create outfits that were feminine and untailored. With cardigan-style jackets and plain or pleated short skirts, solid-colored and patterned wool jersey tops, and horizontal stripes, her designs were the epitome of modern chic. Flannel blazers, delicately embroidered and with a saddle-style double belt, were worn with open-necked blouses and the sailor collar. Her clothes presaged sportswear with her love of muted colors like gray and beige.

LEFT Fortuny's famous Delphos gown, from 1907, a columnar dress of thin silk satin, loosely twisted and pleated, was draped from the shoulder and inspired by the chitons of ancient Greece.

FORTUNY HALLMARKS:

- Batwing sleeves laced along the top
- Hems weighted with Venetian glass or wooden beads
- Silk screening on seams and along edges of dresses to produce a showy effect
- Hand printing (*pochoir*) method used on cotton, velvet, and silk
- Sleeveless Peplos and Delphos vertically pleated dresses, belted with a knotted cord
- Velvet garments, stenciled and overlaid with gold and silver
- Moorish capes and Persian jackets

Modernism and Geometrics

LEFT AND FAR LEFT A late-1920s silk serpentine-print dress. Although it is by an unknown designer, the graphic interlocking snakelike print and sharp curved lines that drape the form clearly reference modernism. Note the asymmetrical draped collar and the buttoned-waist detail.

The turn of the century launched a new machine age, with the development of the automobile, the airplane, and much faster steamship travel. These were all innovations that had a tangible effect not only on the choice of fabrics, design, and colors used but also on the easy-to-wear fashions of the time. Designers created styles that catered to the cosmopolitan woman – "shipboard smartness" and "Riviera chic," as *Vogue* dubbed them in 1926.

The flat, straight-up-and-down dresses of the 1920s were perfect for the stylized geometric-patterned prints that defined the modernist period. Influenced by the cubist and futurist art movements, their dynamic uneven designs, straight lines, spirals, cones, and zigzags were all incorporated into the fashions of the day. Cubist abstract motifs were sewn onto dresses and evening coats. Horizontal stripes were juxtaposed with triangles on dresses, with the same pattern lining the coat. Embroidered circles and triangles in silver and gold thread brought to life the popular black evening dresses of the day, and diagonal patterns with shadings from black to gray produced amazing graphic designs from the prevailing art deco style.

Jean Patou's famous sweaters, with their cubist-style blocks of contrasting color in horizontal stripes inspired by the paintings of Picasso and Braque, were worn by the *beau monde*. Cubist pieces were all the rage, as were Egyptian-style motifs, with serpent designs, hieroglyphics, and scarabs either appliquéd or embroidered onto day and evening dresses.

The modernist designers often concentrated on purifying form and cut: Vionnet, Lanvin, and Chanel controlled the amount of ornamentation they used and, like the cubists, were more interested in form and design. Lucien Lelong's *ligne kynetique* was a range of severely tailored cloth dresses in two shades of jersey with a pared-down simple shape that suggested movement in the design.

Pleats and tucks were often executed as designs in themselves. Treated geometrically, there were

OPPOSITE Actress Marion Morehouse (the poet e. e. cummings's wife) models a one-shouldered bias-cut silk-satin sheath gown with a diagonally cut drop-bodice and slim skirt wrapped to form a two-layered hemline, by Callot Soeurs, 1924.

LEFT Barrel-shaped dress
by Henri Bendel, New York,
First World War period.
Henri Bendel was an
importer, designer, and
fashion writer. His top-line
shop began as an import
house that sold original
designs by such couturiers
as Chanel, Molyneux, and
Schiaparelli, as well as its
own-label versions.

perpendicular tucks in all directions – suits with horizontal pleats on the bodice and vertical pleating on the skirt were popular and contributed to the modernist rectangular look.

The color palette

Contrasting colors in the bold palette of the fauve painters was characteristic of the modernist look. Black-and-white was one of the smartest of color schemes, and part of the avant-garde that dominated fashion at that time introduced neutral gray and beige. Other color combinations – red and green; black, red, and orange; and acid green and cerise pink – were popular art deco colors. Black was often used as a background for bright motifs – black taffeta dresses with red, green, and mauve embroidery on collars and circular panels of embroidery on the skirt, for example. Contrasting hues of different browns and grays on a black background gave clothes a graphic look.

The influence of sportswear

"Sportswear has more to do than anything else with the evolution of the modern mode," said *Vogue* in 1926 – and indeed the functional design of sports clothes was a perfect template for the casual sportswear styles of the new age.

The nautical colors navy, red, and white were incorporated into jersey tunics and sailor-style dresses with navy trimming. Knitwear, sporty cardigans, and pullovers – lightweight and often made of cotton or spun silk, solid-colored or striped and sometimes with decorative nautical motifs – were ultramodern in feel. Jean Patou's sportswear, particularly his outfit for tennis champion Susanne Lenglen, with its pleated shift dress and sleeveless buttoned-down sweater, was a prototype for the fashions to come.

RIGHT Silk white-and-navy dress with triangle detailing from the 1920s exhibits the fascination with clean modernist geometry.

ABOVE, LEFT, AND FAR LEFT
Front, back, and detail
views of a 1905 tulle net
evening dress with pink
velvet-flocked irises and
sequins, designer unknown.
Such delicate flocking
was highly unusual this
early in the century.

Fabrics and Decoration

The other decorative arts and fashion fused during the 1920s to usher in a flamboyant look, and the simplicity of the cut and shape of the clothes was offset by elaborate surface decoration. Technical developments within the textile industry led to the creation of new fabrics, and mass-produced rayon dresses with the appearance of silk were popular for both daywear and eveningwear. Meyer artificial silks and woolens (Pelgram & Meyer, founded in the 1870s, was a well-known American silk mill) were available in a variety of weaves, colors, and textures.

During the day, women would wear angular styles in practical materials like jersey, silk twill, mohair, Kasha, and rayon. Dresses in coarsely woven silk, jersey cardigans, lightweight tweeds, and handwoven brocades were considered chic.

Fluttery evening dresses in flimsy materials like crepe satin and crepe georgette shimmered with diamanté. Dresses using the shiny side of the satin for the trimming and the dull side for the body section could be seen everywhere, and silk was worn in combination with cotton. Silver, gold, and colored lace were often combined with satin, lamé, taffeta, crepe de chine, and georgette. Sumptuous lamé gowns of green and gold, worn with pearls and overlaid with thin lace, shone in the night, as did acid-green moiré tubular dresses. Mariano Fortuny's hand-stenciled velvet coats and dresses woven with shimmering metallic thread were inspired by sixteenth-century velvets, and his motifs and patterns reflected paintings of that period.

Surface decoration and trimmings

The tubular-shaped dresses of the day were an ideal surface for embroidery and other decoration. Appliqué, flocking, raised cord, metal, and contrasting thread, particularly gold and silver, were all seen in dresses following art deco styles. Silver embroidery livened up black chiffon dresses, and embroidered bands were used to trim décolletage and boleros.

Paquin's gowns of green chiffon embroidered with pearls and gold threads on a Chinese design, with bands of embroidery forming the dropped waist, were seen on the pages of *Vogue*. Embroidery silk threads added glamour, and diamanté embroidery for evening was said to be so "brilliant" that the nightclubs hardly needed lighting. Beaded embroidery – creating motifs, lines, or trimmings – was used on most eveningwear.

Oriental, cubist, and floral appliqué provided a decorative surface design technique, and gold and silver leather appliqué added dimension and texture to the background fabric. The beaded evening dress of the Roaring '20s is the signature vintage garment. Designed to be "brilliant," some dresses were completely covered in brightly colored glass beads or

LEFT Sequins, beads, and appliqué on a skirt from the 1920s. Sequins at this time were sometimes made of wax, and easily melted. In gowns, you may find deterioration of the sequins where a dancing partner's hands would rest.

LEFT Ornate beadwork with lace and flower appliqué on a satin bridal gown, 1905.

LEFT A 1928 Vionnet garment decorated with a stylized rose by the design house Lesage. Masterly shading is achieved by strategic use of subtly different colors. Lesage has been creating haute couture embroidery since 1924, and many designers have built a piece or a collection around a Lesage motif.

actual gems like crystal and jet – black beads from coral or glass. These could be sewn onto lightweight silk, rayon, crepe, or chiffon for a striking look.

White crepe georgette dresses with diamanté beads and paillettes were common. Black chiffon dresses with silver and gold beads were particularly spectacular, and whole skirts edged with crystal beads in the same color or edged with rhinestone embroidery sparkled. The craze for sequins was a hallmark of the decade, as they reflected light and could be overlapped to produce linear patterns.

Dresses were as diverse as everything else. White crepe de chine dresses were fringed with chatelaine, and dresses with three-tiered fringe, the top layer of the fringe outlining the bolero top, created a swaying flounced shape. Wide fringed scarves gave extra motion to the silhouette. Feathers were attached to the bodices and skirts of dresses and even featured as headgear.

Further ornamentation was evident in ruffles, sewn in even tiers and along the edges of skirts and pullovers. Bows were worn at the neck and hip and down the front and back of dresses, and lingerie touches at the neck and sleeves were popular. Leather – sometimes metallized – and fur trimmings on cuffs, collars, and hems were key details. For the ultra-glam woman, fur-lined and fur-trimmed gold lamé coats were a must.

Notable designers

Certain couturiers and designers of the period were notable not only for their expertise in design but also for their use of embellishment. Lanvin was known for her spectacular beading techniques and innovative surface embellishment; her free-flowing ribbons at the neck or hip of the dress, petals and ruffles and delicate appliqué in pastel colors – especially Lanvin blue – and her elaborate embroideries were largely inspired by exotic travel.

Callot Soeurs' dresses in embroidered satin or velvet with Eastern motifs in kingfisher blue and black with gold and copper highlights were worn by society girls, as were their silver and gold lamé evening dresses and decorative dragon and paisley medallion motifs. The sisters – Marie Callot Gerber, Marthe Callot Bertrand, Regina Callot Tennyson-Chantrell and Joséphine Callot Crimont, who formed the house in 1895 and who were authorities on antique lace – combined unusual materials such as rubberized gabardine or calfskin with gossamer silks worked with bands of gold lace or silk flowers.

Artist-designer Mary Monaci Galenga's Moyen Age tea gown with a square- or V-neck and tabard was a must-have of the time. Made of silk velvet or crepe de chine, the gown had panels of floating chiffon set into the side seams and was strewn with large Venetian-glass millefiori beads. It also featured gold or silver stenciling in different tones and a variety of patterns.

LEFT AND BELOW American ribbonwork dress, late 1920s, with scalloped hem.

OPPOSITE Mary Monaci Galenga stenciled crimson velvet, 1920s. Born in 1880, Galenga was a mentor of the Italian futurists and developed the technique of stenciling gold onto velvet. A contemporary of Fortuny, she was by 1914 making clothes and textiles. Both Fortuny and Galenga were known for their Renaissance-revival designs.

OPPOSITE INSET Fortuny seashell-stencil turquoise velvet, 1920s. His stenciled velvets have the look of antique frescoes, achieving multiple layers of pigment.

New Silhouettes

The fashions of the 1910s are the sartorial missing link between the belle époque (1890-1914) and the modern fashion of the 1920s. The Edwardian S-bend silhouette made way for the less restrictive empire line with raised waist (1908), followed by the dropped waist (1920s), in which the waist and bosom simply vanished.

The empire line and the hobble skirt

By 1908 social mores were beginning to relax, and this could be seen in the changing silhouette of women's fashions. When Paul Poiret introduced his empire line in that same year, it was greeted with great enthusiasm. Characterized by the columnar silhouette and a slim skirt, his empire-style dresses revived a silhouette last seen in the time of Napoleon. The waistline crept up from the waist to below the bosom, and the hemline rose slightly accordingly. With the waist no longer the focal point, the dresses were suspended from the shoulders.

Loosely cut sleeves and crossed bodices were seen in evening dresses, and the evening coats were based on simple wraps with batwing sleeves. These basic shapes then became starting points that the designers could use for their increasingly opulent styles. Fur trimmings were very popular and served as the new status symbol.

Couturier Jacques Doucet's empire dresses were made of airy fabrics and had intricate floral details showing the influence of art nouveau's decorative language. Free-flowing, with a simple construction, they were made in one piece and fell straight down, which respected the natural form.

Paul Poiret introduced the hobble skirt in 1910, a return to female imprisonment, as women's legs were clamped together in a skirt that was unfeasibly narrow from the knees to the ankles, causing women to walk like Japanese geishas. Yet it proved a short-lived trend – freedom was the new buzzword.

The wartime crinoline

The long, clinging high-waisted dresses were swept away during the First World War when the chemise dress appeared. Pioneered by Lanvin, Worth, and Paquin, the chemise was cut loose and full and was belted under the bosom. Skirts rose suddenly to just above the ankle and filled out. More romantic in style, these new skirts were flared, and although they had layers of petticoats underneath – sometimes to crinoline proportions – they were easy to walk in.

The bodices of dresses were unfitted, and the bust was flat. Women started to wear open-necked blouses, which combined fashion and function, as everything was now loose and biased toward freedom of movement. They were simple and elegant, made in velvet for the afternoon and tinted tulles and muslins for the evening.

There was a brief return to fullness in 1917 with the "barrel skirt," launched by couturiers such as Callot Soeurs, Doeuillet, and Paquin. Cut wide over the hip, it had the pannier look – pulled out at the hips – of a bygone age, sometimes with two or three tiers.

Postwar fashions

After the war fashion did not quite know what direction it should take. The greater freedom women had enjoyed meant that fashion could not go backward. Easy-to-wear elegance became the order of the day, although for the first half of the 1920s sudden changes of line or length of skirt were usual, and the hemline rose and fell in an erratic manner.

Coco Chanel and Jean Patou championed the shorter length, with their forward-looking jersey suits and sporty style. Although in 1919 the hemline rose again and the look of the '20s flapper was nascent, most women still wore widish peg-top skirts and A-line styles – only slightly shorter than before. Jeanne Lanvin's new fluffed-up crinolines were the exception to the slimmer silhouette.

In 1920 an unprecedented mid-calf hemline came in at seven inches above the ankle and with dresses high-waisted. But a year later, hemlines dropped again, practically to the ankle. The longer skirts were circular in cut, and dresses and tops were loosely belted just below the natural waistline and above the hip. Eveningwear was still elaborately trimmed, with fringe all the rage.

From 1922 to 1924, hemlines were four to five inches from the ankle, and the focus was on a vertical silhouette; this was achieved by dropping the waistline dramatically to the hip and with vertically striped tunics or vertical pleats and tucks.

The two-piece came into fashion. This consisted of a blouse or pullover and skirt combination, the top completely unfitted and worn over the skirt to just below hip level, sometimes with a wide belt or sash. Along with ensemble dresses, which consisted of a matched dress and jacket, these were strong fashions, lasting throughout the 1920s. The bateau neckline – slashed straight from one shoulder to the other – was popular, as were scooped necks, V-necks, sailor collars, and three-quarter-length sleeves.

"Paris agrees to disagree about the length of skirts," said *Vogue* in 1923, as designers could not make up their minds how much leg to show. Some women loved Chanel's shorter skirt – a radical nine to ten inches off the ground; others preferred Edward Molyneux's longer Egyptian sheaths, which were almost ankle length.

OPPOSITE Ladies' 1920s daywear with dropped-waist dresses and pleated skirts with jackets, worn with cloche hats. The hemlines are high at just below the knee.

ABOVE Jeanne Lanvin fashion drawing, 1928, "Under the Eyes of New York Skyscrapers," from *Femina* magazine.

ABOVE, LEFT AND RIGHT
Beaded gold and cream
straight-line 1926 flapper
dress, without and with the
jacket. The geometric
diamond design is classic art
deco. The neckline is a
V-neck with fill-in, and the
irregular hem falls to the
knees, typical of the period.

The Age of the Flapper

By 1924 the wisecracking flappers were known as much for their reckless behavior as for their style. Smoking and putting their makeup on in public, the bright young things drank and danced the shimmy and the bunny hug in a frenzy of excitement. Taping up their breasts to get rid of unwanted curves, they looked youthful and boyish, and the new silhouette was slender, straight up and down like a board, and in fact became known as "la garçonne."

As if to herald the new mood, the waistline dropped dramatically in 1925 to below the hip; by 1927 it had disappeared altogether and the hemline had risen a scandalous 15 inches to just below the knee. The flapper look was at its apogee, and extremely short skirts were worn day and night. But hemlines crashed down along with Wall Street in 1929, just as waistlines and busts edged their way into fashion consciousness.

Flapper dresses were straight, loose, and sleeveless, revealing a new body awareness. Arms were bare, and legs and backs were exposed for the first time, becoming new erogenous zones. The illusion of nudity was heightened by the use of diaphanous fabrics and little adornment. Beading was used to emphasize the see-through materials and catch the light, yet also highlighted the risqué nature of the outfits.

The short shift dress, which fell straight down from the shoulders and stopped above the knees, dominated the mid- to late 1920s. Ornamented with geometric and abstract designs, the chemise was often beaded with bands of glittering sequins.

For daywear the three-piece jersey suit was the cornerstone of female fashion: A blouse worn with a patterned or plain knitted sweater or a Chanel-style cardigan jacket with pockets was teamed with a narrow, short, pleated skirt. Day dresses were simple or decorated with details such as horizontal tucks, seaming, or bias-cut panels and square boatnecks. Combinations of fabrics were used, and two-tone

LEFT AND BELOW RIGHT
Molyneux orange silk 1925 dress with silver and gold embroidery. Even in flapper dresses Molyneux's designs were more minimalist than those of his contemporaries. Robust fabrics, strong modernist motifs, and a perfect cut made them demanding though utterly elegant pieces.

SIGNATURE FLAPPER ELEMENTS:

- Uneven split hems and handkerchief points that are longer at the back
- Egyptian- and art-deco-inspired motifs
- Visible seam decoration and double seams
- Diagonal lines and asymmetrical trimmed necklines
- Pockets, buttons, and belts
- Pleated panels on skirts and knife pleats
- Day dresses belted around the hips
- Low-cut necks and backs, with thin straps
- Narrow trailing scarves, sometimes attached to dresses

graded shades were popular, as were mannish suits, ties, and small geometric prints.

A pioneer with Coco Chanel of the "garçonne" look, Jean Patou designed sports ensembles with gradating stripes that could be worn with his geometric pullovers and cardigans on the Riviera. He designed beige three-piece jersey suits, dresses, and wraps. His afternoon flapper-style crepe dresses had self-tied shoulder bows or decorative seams worked in zigzags.

The bright young things wore slacks at home in the early evenings or at the beach. Loosely cut, with drawstring or elasticized waists, these were sometimes called Oxford Bags and fastened at the side for modesty. Paquin's Chinese-printed satin pajamas with embroidered satin jacket were all the rage.

The perfectly straight-line collarless coat, which buttoned at the waist like a cardigan jacket, and a high-collar coat with a sash at the waist maintained their popularity, as did the slightly circular coat with fur collar that wrapped over on the diagonal, fastening with a single loop and button at hip level.

Eveningwear

The modern social whirl of cabarets, masquerade parties, and dancing gave rise to more extravagant eveningwear. By 1928 Paris was determined to abandon the tubular dresses, and floating panels and Vionnet's bias-cut dresses, which followed the contours of the body, became popular. Draperies from the hips gave the illusion of length and fullness, and movement was added with attached panels or uneven hemlines. Chanel's black evening dresses with huge transparent draperies, Paquin's acid-green moiré dresses with a V-neck and bulk at the hip, and Molyneux's transparent printed dresses with full, scalloped skirts and arm draperies are all significant flapper styles.

Crystal-beaded waves with coral fish and lilac flamingos in lotus ponds were some of Molyneux's unconventional surface decoration on flapper dresses. He experimented with ostrich feathers and buttons resembling cigarette butts or lipsticks, and his beaded chemises are some of the most exquisite.

OPPOSITE Model Dinarzade wearing a sleeveless shiny dress with V-neck, dropped waist, and flaring skirt with designs at the hem, by Edward Molyneux, 1924.

ABOVE Silver lamé flower-patterned Erté-style dress with a flower corsage at the waist, early 1920s.

LEFT AND ABOVE RIGHT Cream and white 1925 beaded flapper dress in starburst art deco design.

◄Beading and fringe
Evening dresses with sequins, feathers, and other ornate surface decorations were characteristic of the period, as in this fringed flapper dress, seen here modeled by Joan Crawford in the 1920s.

The sheath dress
The slinky sheath was made of chiffon, silk, or crepe de chine and clung to the female form from shoestring shoulder straps.

▼Geometrics
Sweeping bold, curved patterns in deep colors, which included dramatic red, black, and blue, appeared from 1910, along with other geometric patterns and cubist motifs.

Key looks of the era
1900–1929

Edwardian blouses
The Edwardian blouse, made of lace with ruffles, or striped and purposeful, epitomized the dual femininity – both demure and assertive – of the times.

S-shaped corsets
The early-century corset created the idealized female form with a tiny waist – achieved through artificial distortion of the body.

Style Russe
Chanel's early 1920s Russian style, attributed to her liaison with Russian Grand Duke Dmitri, consisted of tunic shapes, fur trimmings, and embroidery. This look reflected the influx of Russians to Paris after the Revolution. "Style Russe" would be revisited by many designers, as in Saint Laurent's "Russian Revolution" in the mid-1970s.

▲Hobble and kite dresses
After the emancipation from the strict S-bend silhouette, dresses became looser while the hobble, as created by Paul Poiret, was groundbreaking in developing the narrow, shorter hemline – an influence that can be seen in these kite dresses from 1918. Lace-up boots also came back into fashion during the years of the First World War.

Dropped waist

[c]urves and the hourglass figure [w]ere out, and belts, sashes, or [tie]s were worn around the hips. [T]he waist disappeared to create [th]e fashionable beanpole look [b]eloved in the 1920s, as typified [in] the illustration from Mab [P]atterns, April 1925, below.

La garçonne look

A new androgyny accompanied the flapper era, and women wore short hair and dresses that were straight and loose and revealed bare arms. The lithe, athletic modern form was the new sexy look.

YOU WILL FIND THE PATTERN DETAILS ON THE LAST EDITORIAL PAGE.

Velvets and furs

Fur coats, or coats trimmed in fur, were popular. Many had a single large button, or simply wrapped over a shawl collar, wide cuffs, and fell to the knees. Velvet was also used in jackets, wraps, and dresses; the sumptuous material was part of the style of opulence and the luxury of art deco fashion.

▲Kimono style

Japanese-style dresses were seen as very exotic and heralded a new form of beauty based on simplicity and oriental design. Many tea gowns, like the 1925 dress above, had the square-cut sleeves and shape of the kimono.

▲Bare backs and bias cuts

Cut on the bias, the new body-hugging dresses seemed to spiral around the body and moved with the wearer. Backless dresses, like the 1929 version above, with or without trains, began to make an appearance later in the 1920s.

Sweaters

Silk or wool, and striped, plain, or with *trompe l'oeil* motifs, the pullover was a key element in flapper style of the 1920s.

Slacks

Bright young things in the 1920s would wear silken pajamas and sailor pants for early evening or as fashionable resort wear.

1930s

Epitomized by the elongated draped gowns worn by movie stars, the 1930s will forever be remembered as the era of Hollywood glamour. Liberated from the corsets and cumbersome designs of previous years, women were now able to dress in a way that was both stylish and practical, while new fabrics encouraged designers to experiment with original looks.

Form was more important than detail and embellishment as designers focused on the silhouette. Unlike the boyish 1920s, when breasts were strapped down and dresses were loose and boxy, clothes were cut to follow the lines of the body, showing off the female figure in a more provocative manner than ever before. Shoulders were bared in the first halter-neck and backless gowns, and the bias-cut dress – pioneered by Parisian couturier Madeleine Vionnet – clung to every curve. Suits consisted of neat-fitting, waist-length jackets with skirts to mid-calf. Coco Chanel designed two-piece suits in wool jersey fabrics, heralding a sportier look, which became a surprise daywear hit.

However, many of these new trends were born of necessity. Coming between the two World Wars and directly after the stock market crash of 1929, times were hard. The Great Depression obliged designers to work with cheaper materials, and ordinary women could no longer afford the sartorial excesses of previous decades. Even the wealthiest showed restraint in what they wore, while screen idols such as Katharine Hepburn and Bette Davis represented a glamour that most could only dream of.

Daywear Fashions

Until the 1930s, daywear had often been more decorative than practical. But now, for the first time, women of all social backgrounds were beginning to lead busier and more productive lives, and so clothes became easy to wear and unrestrictive. Although eveningwear had a strong element of escapist glamour, by day, elegant and neat clothes were key.

Money was tight, so women were no longer at liberty to indulge their every fashion fancy and had to find other ways to look smart. Clothes were mended instead of replaced, and accessories played an important part. Costume jewelry, especially brooches, earrings, and rings, was favored as a cheaper alternative to the priceless gems that had previously been the required jewelry among the fashionable classes. Fine leather gloves in suede or lambskin also added an essential touch to daywear. Hats were worn at a fashionable tilt, and while the beret replaced the cloche hat, pillboxes also became popular, and the turban emerged as one of the most glamorous accessories of the time.

As the decade progressed, function became more and more important, and by the time the Second World War had begun in Europe in 1939, simple clothes such as slacks, sweaters, classic shirtwaist dresses, and low-heeled shoes were the staple of most women's wardrobes. Designers began to adapt the mood of their collections to more military-inspired, square-shouldered clothing, with skirts that hung just below the knee and often slightly longer at the back.

But this new liking for practical day clothes did not mean that fashion had lost its femininity; on the contrary, designers compensated by creating a more hourglass silhouette. Instead of sitting low on the hips as they had in the 1920s, waistlines returned to the natural waist, if not slightly higher, and were often cinched-in to create a more curvaceous figure. Necklines were lowered and frequently had wide scalloped edges and ruffled collars, while the jabot blouse – with its ornamental cascade of ruffles down the front – became hugely fashionable, as did the pussycat-bow neckline.

Flamboyant floral and geometric prints were favorites for blouses and day dresses, while the most fashionable colors of the time were powder blue, maize, gray, navy, green, brown, and red. Rose was popular among teenage girls, while black was generally reserved for eveningwear.

Accents were important too: Belts and sashes were wide, buttons were bold, and silk flowers were substantial yet always in proportion to the jacket or dress they were adorning.

ABOVE AND LEFT Blouse with jabot collar and trumpet sleeves by Edward Molyneux, mid-1930s. The sleeves feature lengths of rouleau, in which the material is rolled and applied to net, a typical 1930s techique.

PAGE 36 White organza 1938 bridesmaid's dress sprinkled with flowers by Jeanne Lanvin, worn with a wide-brimmed organza hat with streamers, in front of a backdrop of line drawings of moths.

OPPOSITE A 1932 illustration depicting 1930s day dresses by, from left to right, Goupy, Worth, Augustabernard, and Schiaparelli.

ABOVE White crepe dress with swooped sleeves and bodice by Maggy Rouff, 1932.

LEFT Black suit with white, jabotlike lapels, by Molyneux, 1938. A master of subdued elegance in both his daywear and his eveningwear, Molyneux catered to the highest social circles. The saucer hat is decorated with lilies of the valley.

Day suits were revolutionized by Coco Chanel, who saw the affordable yet fashionable potential of wool jersey cloth. In the United States the Tirocchi sisters, who were loved for their afternoon dresses and eveningwear, also used wool jersey fabrics for suiting. The Tirocchis were the couturiers of choice for those who could afford the luxury of made-to-measure fashions. Creating unique pieces for their customers, they – like Chanel – were fond of sportswear. With the introduction of their wide-legged, pajama-style slacks, they were trendsetters in the move toward softer and sportier tailoring and reflected the more active lifestyle that women were embracing.

The promotion of fitness and a slim figure, begun in the 1920s, gathered momentum in the United States and Europe. In Britain, in 1930, the Women's League of Health and Beauty was founded; its motto was "Movement is life." Women began to enjoy a more outdoor life, and sunworshiping became a common leisure pursuit. Beach wraps, carryalls, soft hats, and knitted bathing suits were all objects of desire for the summer season. Swimwear became briefer and more risqué as the backs were scooped out so that women could develop tanned backs to show off at night in backless gowns. In keeping with these new freedoms, corsets, although still available, were eschewed in favor of bras and girdles, while silk and rayon stockings began to replace woolen ones.

Living proof that fashion and an active life could go hand in hand, celebrated American aviator Amelia Earhart became as iconic a figure as any of the Hollywood film stars of the time. Earhart always removed her goggles immediately upon landing and refused to don typical aviation gear. Instead, she wore elegantly tailored flying suits, silk neck scarves, and wide-legged slacks, all of which spawned a multitude of high-fashion replicas.

How to keep up with the new fashions depended a lot on where one lived. In the United States, where ready-to-wear clothing was a well-established industry, most women brought their clothes from department stores or from mail-order catalogs, which served the millions who lived in remote areas. Some made their own clothes, from paper patterns, as did most women in Britain, where ready-to-wear was in its infancy. Only the rich could afford Paris couture.

LEFT This early-1930s printed chiffon dress by the house of Paquin, with a gold lamé slip and irregular hem, looks amazingly contemporary. The waist detail and pleating serve as anchors for the flying panels of chiffon layering the skirt.

Fabrics and Prints

Although the 1930s witnessed a great economic depression, it was still a period of industrial advances, as machinery and techniques that were developed before, during, and after the First World War began to have an effect on everyday life. Fashion benefited from many new inventions, such as zippers and rayon – the first commercially used man-made fiber. In 1935 the DuPont de Nemours Company successfully synthesized nylon, and this sparked a major trend for nylon stockings, which quickly replaced the woolen versions formerly worn. The arrival of these washable, easy-care fabrics was heavily marketed by manufacturers and was greeted with great excitement by fashion designers and housewives alike.

In the mood of financial restraint that characterized the decade, designers also began to experiment with fabrics previously not considered appropriate for mainstream dressmaking. In women's suiting, Coco Chanel pioneered the use of cotton and wool jersey, a fabric that had previously been used predominantly for men's underwear. Her soft, fitted two-piece suits quickly became the toast of Parisian fashion and kick-started the vogue for less formal attire. But while these new fabrics took hold, soft crepe, chiffon, and satin were still frequently used, and pure silk continued to be the most desirable fabric, as it lent itself perfectly to the folds and drapes of 1930s couture.

Because of the numerous improvements in mass-production techniques during the 1930s, a wider range of women had gained access to well-made and well-cut clothes. However, the advent of war in Europe in 1939 brought that temporarily to an end, preventing civilian access to clothing manufacturers for several years while much of the world focused on the war effort.

Fastenings

Originally known as the "slide fastener," the zipper was invented as far back as 1893, but in its early days it was used only to fasten footwear. When it was finally adopted by the clothing industry in the 1930s, it became an instant hit in all areas of fashion design. A sales campaign was mounted for children's clothing, praising the zipper for promoting self-reliance in youngsters because it made it possible for them to dress themselves. In 1937 the zipper beat the button in the "Battle of the Fly," when tailors raved over its usefulness in men's trousers.

The popularity of the zipper continued to grow during the 1930s, and it was quickly embraced by womenswear designers. Many designers, including Elsa Schiaparelli, even featured it as an aesthetic detail, sometimes running it through the back of a dress or simply leaving it unconcealed. The predominance of zippers in manufactured clothing increased toward the end of the decade, primarily as side-closing fasteners.

Buttons too became part of surface decoration, with designers considering the fastening as part and parcel of the design. Schiaparelli created insect, flower, and lip buttons and others in Dalí-esque and whimsical shapes. By this point Bakelite plastic was cheap and fashionable and could be easily molded; it was particularly well suited to art deco shapes. Black and brown Bakelite were the most common colors, but lighter colors were developed during the 1930s. Lucite, a clear, hard resin invented in 1931, was also used to make buttons during this period.

The new emphasis was on looking chic in a way that was practical for everyday life, and this was reflected not just in the fastenings and materials used but also in the cut and patterns of the clothes themselves.

Cutting techniques and dress patterns

The tricks of draping and intricate seaming first learned in the 1920s were now applied to making dresses that clung to the body, creating the streamlined chic that characterized the decade. In addition, a new way of cutting fabric was invented by Parisian designer Madeleine Vionnet. Her bias-cut technique enabled women, for the first time, to wear clothes that clung flirtatiously to the figure and showed off the body in a more naturalistic way than ever before. At the same time, necklines were lowered, while torsos were sensuously molded beneath squared shoulders. For evening the bare back became the new erogenous zone, replacing the legs of the 1920s.

At the beginning of the decade, hemlines dropped dramatically to the ankle, and they remained there until the end of the 1930s. Skirts were designed with great detail. Upper-skirt yokes appeared for the first

OPPOSITE A selection of print textiles exhibiting the fascination with Art Deco – the two left top and bottom are earlier than the two right top and bottom. The lower right is a souvenir shirt from the maiden voyage of the Queen Mary, 1936.

FEATURES OF 1930S PRINTS:

❖ Designs printed on silk, rayon, and crinkle crepe
❖ Bold lines and patterns of the prevailing art deco style
❖ Graphic designs and lettering, polkadots and hand-drawn circles, bold florals
❖ Contrasting colors and bright shades to emphasize print
❖ Picture prints, such as cars, animals, and popular objects
❖ Influences from cubism and artists such as Picasso and Man Ray

time, designed in a V shape and extending from one hip to the center of the yoke, then continuing to the opposite hip. Layered and ruffled looks appeared on skirts, sometimes in tiers. The skirt bottom was often full, with pleats or gathers. Soft gathers replaced darts, dress waists returned to the natural waistline, and moderately full skirts accentuated a small waist and minimized the hips. Dress bodices were designed with inset pieces and yokes that provided extra interest. Necklines received dramatic attention by designers, often with wide scallop-edged or ruffled collars. Arms also took on a new importance as designers experimented with new shapes such as voluminous puffed or flared sleeves.

Prints and surface decoration

As a continuation of the art deco styles popular in the 1920s, embroidery and appliqué continued to be favored as a decorative touch on cardigans, blouses, and dresses. These designs were often highly detailed, featuring small-scale floral motifs and more animated subjects such as show horses, kittens, and cars. Lamé became a fashionable yarn for eveningwear and was used as often as a detail in embroidery as it was throughout an entire piece of cloth. Textile design in general became more interesting as polkadots, geometric patterns, and colorful prints became de rigueur.

There was a great cross-fertilization of visual ideas from such artists as Salvador Dalí, Jean Cocteau, Alberto Giacometti, and Marcel Vertes, whose work influenced not just print and textile designs but also embroidery and jewelry.

Furs and trimmings

During this era, fur of all kinds was worn extensively in winter, both by day and at night. Fur capes, coats, stoles, wraps, accessories, and trimmings completed women's outfits. Pelts in demand were sable, mink, chinchilla, Persian lamb, and silver fox.

RIGHT Embroidery sample by Lesage, created for Elsa Schiaparelli's Circus collection – the perfect marriage of a master embroiderer and a visionary couturier.

RIGHT 1936 Schiaparelli garment with a mad profusion of beaded decoration by the design house Lesage.

RIGHT Embroidery detail from a 1930s evening jacket. The unusual wheat motif in raised gold leather is typical of the decorative avant-garde style of Elsa Schiaparelli.

OPPOSITE Rayon dresses designed by Lucien Lelong, from a fashion plate in *Femina* magazine, 1935. Rayon was the decade's most prominent fabric achievement, providing the feel of silk in an easy-care material.

Elsa Schiaparelli and Coco Chanel

Arguably the two most important designers of the 1930s, Elsa Schiaparelli (1896-1973) and Coco Chanel (1883-1971) could not have been more different. Schiaparelli created high-octane, almost shocking clothes in bright colors and with groundbreaking textile designs and an exaggerated silhouette. Chanel designed easy-to-wear clothes in a palette of black, white, and beige. Considering their opposing aesthetic values, it is hard to imagine that these couturiers could have thrived alongside each other in Paris during the same decade. Today Chanel remains one of the most successful luxury brands of all times while Schiaparelli's name endures only in fashion history. But in the 1930s they enjoyed equal fame and were the greatest of rivals.

Barely five feet tall, Schiaparelli had always been told that she was ugly. Her garments were high-waisted, broad-shouldered, and designed to elongate the figure – an aesthetic evidently formed to suit her own sartorial tastes and requirements. Chanel, on the other hand, owed a certain amount of her success to her good looks. The embodiment of her brand with her slim, boyish figure, cropped hair, and tanned skin, she became an ideal for a generation of women.

Ten years older than Schiaparelli, Chanel rose to professional distinction against far greater odds. Her mother died when she was six years old, and the rest of her childhood was spent in an orphanage. During a brief career as a concert-hall singer, Gabrielle – as she was originally named – adopted the name Coco. It was during this time that she became the mistress of a wealthy English industrialist whose connections and financial backing enabled her to open her own millinery shop in 1910.

Born in Rome, Schiaparelli came from a family of moneyed intellectuals. Her father was a scholar in Islamic and Arabic studies and her uncle a renowned astronomer – the influences from her upbringing were regularly apparent in her work, not least in her winter 1938-9 Lucky Stars collection.

The different backgrounds of these two designers were reflected constantly in their attitude toward their work. Chanel regarded couture as a profession, while Schiaparelli always insisted that it was an art. A close friend of Picasso and the surrealist artists Dalí and Man Ray, Elsa was a firm fixture on the early-twentieth-century international arts scene; a book of her poetry was published in 1911. She even managed to bridge the gap between fashion and literature by inventing poetic names for the specific colors she used in her collections – shocking pink was introduced in 1937, while other color names that have became part of our everyday language include royal blue and ice blue.

OPPOSITE Black moiré suit with a crepe black-and-white striped blouse, by Chanel, and a black straw hat with a ribbon chou, 1938.

RIGHT Gabrielle "Coco" Chanel in suit and beret, 1930s. Her unique style of menswear-influenced sporty clothing was meant for modern active women like herself.

Coco Chanel's legacy could not be more evident today, as Karl Lagerfeld, creative director at Chanel since her death, continues to plunder the fashion house's archives, working strictly with her vision in mind. Aside from her iconic Chanel No. 5 perfume, the wool jersey suit is one of her most famous innovations. Comfort was key to her designs, and she is credited with revolutionizing fashion – liberating women from their restrictive corsets and introducing them to a freer, more casual elegance. In stark contrast to the clothing seen in her youth, Chanel said that she wanted to give women "the possibility to laugh and eat without necessarily having to faint." For Schiaparelli, however, comfort and practicality were secondary to fashion. She famously said, "Never fit a dress to the body but train the body to fit the dress."

While Schiaparelli and most other international fashion houses continued to create ankle-length sheath dresses, Chanel seemed uninterested in the more formal etiquette of fashion; her designs were largely limited to daytime or sportswear dresses and suits, which inevitably reached mid-calf in length. Rather than creating the long, bias-cut evening gowns popularized by Hollywood movie stars, she preferred designing more versatile two-piece cocktail suits, which allowed the wearer to go elegantly from early-evening to late-night soirée without having to change outfits.

For Schiaparelli, it was the *trompe l'oeil* "bow" knitted sweaters that effectively launched her career. Her later innovations included the use of zippers as decorative elements, a backless evening gown with a pleated, bustle-like compartment for stashing a flask, and a fabric print composed of newspaper clippings. Her customers needed plenty of confidence, as her clothes were definitely designed to stand out.

Perhaps one of the best examples of her use of color and textiles is a floor-length, harlequin-patterned wool felt coat from her 1939 Commedia dell'Arte collection. Composed of graduated lozenges of primary colors plus black and white,

RIGHT Elsa Schiaparelli, pictured far right with a friend, in her own-designed trousered skirt, Hyde Park, London, 1935.

BELOW Schiaparelli's handknitted woolen pullover launched in 1927 but became a sensational hit in the early 1930s with its allusion to the typical jabot collar of the time. The stepped outline of the bow's curves and the *trompe l'oeil* effect create a strong graphic representation.

LEFT 1938 illustration by Christian Bérard entitled "Revolutionary Red, Ruthlessly Cut" and depicting a Schiaparelli military-inspired red coat over a printed dress. The woman is holding a Schiaparelli hand mask.

Bérard

the faceted patchwork effect is strongly reminiscent of Man Ray's cubist painting *Le Beau Temps*, of the same year. The use of garish color and geometric designcould not have been further from Chanel's "sophisticated" taste.

By the early 1930s Chanel's reputation had grown enormously, and in 1931 she was paid a million dollars by MGM boss Samuel Goldwyn to dress the female stars of many of his motion pictures, including Katharine Hepburn and, later, Grace Kelly and Elizabeth Taylor. Schiaparelli created clothing for many stage productions and films, among them costumes for Mae West in *Every Day's a Holiday* (1937) and Zsa Zsa Gabor in *Moulin Rouge* (1952). Among her regular clients were the Duchess of Windsor, Marlene Dietrich, and Katharine Hepburn.

The Second World War marked the end of Elsa Schiaparelli's business. She retired from fashion, dying in 1973. Coco continued to run her business until her death in 1971, in her residential suite at the Ritz, in Paris.

SIGNATURE SCHIAPARELLI ELEMENTS:

❖ High waistlines
❖ Shoulder pads and broad shoulders
❖ Exaggerated silhouettes, including small bustles
❖ Bright colors, such as shocking pink and royal blue
❖ *Trompe l'oeil* knits
❖ Zippers as decorative elements
❖ Long-line bias-cut dresses
❖ Backless evening gowns
❖ Geometric and Picasso-inspired patterns

ABOVE Floor-length, harlequin wool felt coat from Schiaparelli's 1939 Commedia dell'Arte collection. The striking faceted patchwork effect is strongly reminiscent of the cubist painting *Le Beau Temps* by Man Ray.

Evening Glamour

While Paris couturiers of the 1930s were the driving force behind changing trends, the era is perhaps best exemplified by the Hollywood film stars who brought their clothes to life. Actresses such as Marlene Dietrich, Joan Crawford, and Barbara Stanwyck epitomized the look, with their penchant for elongated bias-cut, halter-neck gowns in shimmering silk fabrics. During this time of economic crisis, when even some of couture's wealthiest customers were forced to rein in their shopping habits, Hollywood became the ultimate showcase for a designer's work.

Depression-weary audiences flocked in record numbers to the movies, hungry for some much-needed glamour and escapism. And although some of the films of the time took on a tone of gritty realism, the leading ladies remained relentlessly stylish and groomed to perfection. Inside these movie theaters existed a world of opulence that most of the audience could only dream of – and the costumes worn had almost as much pulling power as the stars themselves.

Fashion and film joined hands as the same designers who dressed the stars for their red-carpet appearances were also called upon to create costumes for the films they starred in. At Paramount Studios, costume designer Travis Banton brought understated glamour and elegance to actresses such as Mae West and Carole Lombard with his beautifully cut suits and bias-cut dresses. Meanwhile, Gilbert Adrian, head of costume at MGM, created the signature looks of the studio's major stars, including Greta Garbo and Jean Harlow. The broad-shouldered suits in which he dressed Joan Crawford became hugely fashionable, and the puff-sleeved dress that she wore in the 1933 film *Letty Lyndon* sent female members of the audience rushing to their sewing machines to create their own versions of the look.

This was a time before the term *fashion stylist* had even been invented, and Adrian's role in introducing stars to designers was of fundamental importance. Although Madeleine Vionnet is said to have invented the bias cut and Elsa Schiaparelli – who designed clothes for more than 30 films – was credited with inventing padded shoulders, it was Adrian who had the awareness to bring these high-fashion looks to the silver screen. In so doing, he created the style that dominated American fashion during the 1930s. Referring to the suits she wore in some of her films, Joan Crawford praised his emphasis on simplicity and his ability to make a dramatic point through clever costume choices.

ABOVE AND LEFT Green 1939 crepe de chine dress by Jeanne Lanvin, with tie neckline and heavily embroidered balloon sleeves. The dress features typical Lanvin elements – a long, slim silhouette and intricate embellishment in the form of both embroidery and appliqué.

OPPOSITE Crepe dresses by Lucien Lelong, 1935.

ABOVE Black velvet 1930s dress with pink plastic pyramid sequins, pink lining, and closed-wrist fastenings at the cuff of medieval-style sleeves.

Adrian's understanding of light and shadow ensured that the clothes looked as good on black-and-white film as they did in the flesh. A master of form and structure, he had an impeccable eye for perfectly cut clothes and held Parisian couture in the greatest esteem. It was Gilbert who, in 1931, persuaded MGM boss Samuel Goldwyn to pay Coco Chanel a staggering million dollars to provide clothes for the studio's major stars.

But although Gilbert was an undeniably powerful figure in both film and fashion, he nevertheless had rigid guidelines to adhere to when dressing his stars. Bound by what was known as the Hayes Code, costume designers were strictly censored on what they could allow an actress to show. Following the titillating and scandalous films of the 1920s, the 1930s saw a return to modesty, even prudishness, and too much cleavage on display was considered obscene. In order to get around these rules, actresses removed their bras and wore slinky, draped dresses that clung to the body without revealing too much bare flesh. While the conservatives could not complain, the female form was now visible in a more provocative way than ever. And while the cleavage was kept under wraps, designers created dresses to unveil alternative erogenous zones. The halter-neck evening gown made its fashion debut, and – as long as the navel was covered up – bare-midriff top and skirt combinations enjoyed a brief spell of popularity.

While intricate beading, appliqué, and encrusted jewels were often used as features on the sleeve or waistline or as a detail around the back or neckline, for the most part the evening gowns of the 1930s were exquisite by virtue of their simplicity. Gowns were perfectly cut to create the illusion of a long and slender silhouette, often with elongated flared sleeves and exaggerated trains at the back. Fur of all kinds was seen as highly desirable and was worn everywhere by all who could afford it. Wraps and capes were frequently teamed with full-length silk satin evening gloves.

In contrast to the riotous 1920s, the new aesthetic was sophisticated and elegant, and it was not just film stars who put high fashion in the spotlight. Royalty were equally revered; in Britain images of the Duke and Duchess of Windsor, Princess Marina, and the Duchess of York (later Queen Elizabeth, consort of George VI) also filled newsreels and newspapers. The clothes they wore were as much of a talking point as in more recent

RIGHT Black wool coat with ermine fur collar by French label Jenny, 1938.

ABOVE AND RIGHT Net appliqué late-1930s dress with lime underslip and short balloon sleeves, by Jeanne Lanvin.

LEFT AND BELOW Front and back views of a 1930s Paquin chiffon evening gown with an embroidered pattern of silver beading and sequins. The scarlet crepe inserts are a striking color accent and have been cleverly combined with the straps to create tiebacks that define the waist.

years with modern royals such as Diana, Princess of Wales. *Life* magazine featured a story on the Mainbocher blue wedding dress worn by the divorced Mrs. Wallis Simpson, who married the Duke of Windsor in 1937, and the garment won enormous international admiration. Smaller clothing companies, such as Bonwit Teller of Fifth Avenue in New York City, which sold a copy for a tenth of the price, immediately produced it in short-sleeve versions. Within six months the "Wally" dress was available for even less at Lord & Taylor, and finally a mere $8.90 could buy one at Klein's cash-and-carry.

By the 1930s countless fashion houses had come to prominence, and their designs were widely emulated. British-born designer Edward Molyneux, the epitome of cool elegance, became known as the man to whom a woman would turn if she wanted to look absolutely right without being utterly predictable. His clothes can usually be recognized by their understated elegance, and he generally designed evening dresses in a discreet color palette of black, navy, gray, and beige.

Augusta Bernard, who styled her name as one word for her label, Augustabernard, was another fashion designer to enjoy notable success during the decade. She made slim bias-cut evening dresses in pale moonlit colors. Although based in Paris, Bernard had a large American clientele, who found that her simple dresses were an exquisite backdrop for their expensive jewelry.

These designers belonged to an eminent band of Parisian couturiers, which also included Louise Boulanger, Cristóbal Balenciaga, Robert Piguet, and Madeleine Vionnet, all of whom managed to a greater or lesser extent to survive during the difficult years between the First and Second World Wars. Besides serving the social elite of their day, many of these designers became icons in their own right and – no matter what their background – found themselves mingling with stars, aristocracy, and royalty.

The eveningwear styles from the 1930s, perhaps more than those from any other fashion era, continue to directly influence eveningwear designs popular today. The elongated gowns, halter-neck dresses, and draped cowl neckline so frequently seen on the red carpet today owe a great debt to the 1930s. Designers such as John Galliano, Valentino, and Julien Macdonald continue to reference this decade – when Hollywood glamour was born.

▼ Bias-cut gowns

Fabric was cut on the diagonal, allowing dresses to cling naturally to the body. Introduced by Madeleine Vionnet, this was one of the most significant elements of 1930s fashion. Below, a black velvet dress trimmed in ermine and a white crepe and panne velvet dress, both by Vionnet, circa 1930.

▶ Skirts with wedge-cut pleats

Fitted at the hip with yokes, skirts often featured wedge-cut pleats, giving a fullness to the hemline, which ended at mid-calf. The outfit pictured here also exhibits other classic 1930s styles: hat and gloves, neckline bow, and fur stole.

Rayon

The first commercially used man-made fabric was available in several different finishes and was quickly exploited by designers keen to experiment with new textiles.

Key looks of the decade

1930s

Jabot blouse

Decorative ruffles cascaded from the collar down the front of the blouse or dress, becoming a popular style, particularly for daywear.

▶ Sportswear influences

Tailoring took on a sportier feel as Coco Chanel pioneered the use of soft wool jersey fabrics for women's suiting. More women engaged in outdoor activities such as golfing. Here, four women pose with golf clubs wearing beach pajamas in 1935.

◀ Flared sleeves

Narrow-fitting at the shoulder, blouses featured sleeves that widened toward the wrist. These were often exaggerated and elongated on evening gowns.

Costume jewelry

Often made in enamel and glass, costume jewelry such as brooches, bracelets, and beaded necklaces was a fashionable and affordable new look.

Narrow suits worn with a hat and gloves

Slim-fitting tailored suits were a practical look for daywear and were teamed with gloves and hats of various styles.

Zippers

Slide fasteners were a welcome new invention, which quickly replaced buttons in many areas of fashion. Some designers, such as Schiaparelli, even made features of this metal fastening.

◄ Halter-neck backless evening gowns

Backs became the new erogenous zone as designers draped fabric around the neck, leaving shoulders and backs on show, as seen here in a 1935 satin version.

▲ Art deco patterns

Characterized by symmetrical geometric patterns, art deco prints were a leftover trend from the 1920s and were regularly seen on dresses, blouses, and scarves.

◄ Fur

Worn day and night, fur creations of all types were popular luxury items. Capes, coats, stoles, and wraps were made using pelts of ermine, fox, mink, and chinchilla. This ermine version from 1935 has a draped collar.

1940s

Social trends dictate fashion. Nowhere is this more evident than in the 1940s. With the outbreak of war, things changed very quickly. There were shortages of everything and civilian life was taken over and transformed. The conscription of women in Europe and America changed the female role and brought women out of the home to work for the war effort. Materials such as silk and wool were needed for the war. Factories were used for parachutes and other war supplies, so many of the 1940s vintage clothes are made out of rayon, synthetic jersey, and other man-made fabrics. Clothing rationing started in 1941, and the use of trimmings and certain materials was subject to government decree. The nonfashion fashion of the war years resulted in a conservative and military style, yet the tailoring was magnificent — outfits had to last several seasons. British couture was still being made, but only for export to procure much-needed dollars for armaments. France lost its position at the apex of fashion in 1940 under German occupation and did not regain its undisputed leadership until the liberation in 1944, when its couture collection was splendid. Meanwhile, the United States looked to its own designers to create fashions; the functional and easy American ready-to-wear was born with brightly colored playsuits in materials such as gingham and denim. After the war, the direction of fashion was slow to change, especially where rationing was still in place. The American softened silhouette presaged the dramatic New Look unveiled in 1947 by Christian Dior, and the mood changed irrevocably.

The Wartime Silhouette

"Il faut 'skimp' pour être chic" – you must skimp to be chic – declared *Vogue* in October 1941, referring to the tight, short-skirted silhouette that was ushered in that year and greeted with horror by the public. Suddenly the flirty fullness of the 1930s curvy female gave way to an angular, hard silhouette, which, as *Vogue* declared in the same year, "would be brutally unbecoming unless women kept their figures." Driven by the wartime economy, the sculptural silhouette was the result of government rationing. The stiff tailoring, economy of cut, nipped-in waist, and narrow skirts produced a slim shape that de-emphasized the female curves and made the form appear slender yet mannish. Elaboration was out, and pared-down elegance was the order of the day. The silhouette, therefore, inadvertently gave the illusion of brisk competence. And with its "sensible" image, "beauty" was not part of the wartime aesthetic. *Vogue* said in 1942 that it looked, "sharp, cold and even bold."

The lady's suit

The drab uniformity of the war years was mirrored in the severe military-cut suit, which formed the bedrock of wartime fashion. Women wore clothes that were cut along the lines of the uniforms worn by men. Colors such as air-force blue and flag red were used, as these reduced wastage. Military influences were everywhere, from half-belts like those on uniform greatcoats to the padded-shoulder severity of wartime jackets. *Vogue* called it "couture austerity." Driven by necessity rather than by desire, restrictions on materials resulted in a silhouette that became refined and unadorned. Indeed, it was unpatriotic to be concerned with flounces and fripperies.

The suit was cut in a straight, mannish style – often refashioned from the existing male suit – with sharp-edged shoulder pads to give women a brisk no-nonsense air, in keeping with their role as key wartime workers. Boxy, with wide shoulders and barely nipped-in waists, the jackets were short, at 25 inches or less in length. Single-breasted and often unlined – in order to comply with fabric restrictions – they were, however, tailored and well made, for they had to last several seasons. If they were lined, it was often with rayon. To save material, cuffs and patch pockets were banned in America as part of a "no fabric on fabric" rule. Sometimes jacket sleeves were cropped short to reveal the blouse underneath and belts buckled at the back to leave the front smooth. The buttons, restricted to three or fewer, were often covered in the corresponding suit material.

Since wool was impossible to come by, new materials such as thick, heavy rayon took their place. Despite what seems like an era of drab uniformity, a lot of the 1940s export couture suits have clever detailing. Clever paneling, set in different ways, in corded material, for example, and "crenellated" yokes, added a dash of variety to the standard fare. Soft velveteen suits were fashionable and had gored skirts, accompanied by an unlined jacket with a blouse feel. The outfit was completed with platform heels, often in cork or wood.

After the war, the female silhouette, while remaining slim, started to show changes. A softer line was creeping in, with jackets losing the military cut. Gathered and curved-in waistlines, scalloped shoulders, and gathered sleeves were seen in the Sears catalog in 1946, and *Vogue* featured Parisian suits with hip-draped skirts and coat dresses with stand-up collars.

PAGE 60 Red checked dress in spun rayon, 1943. Two staples of the time, rayon and gingham, are used in this 1940s dress with three-quarter-length sleeves, necktie bow, and hip pockets. The model stands in front of an Uncle Sam recruitment poster for the U.S. armed forces.

LEFT Gray wool suit with red trim by American label Foxbrownie, 1944. Foxbrownie (or Fox-Brownie, as it is sometimes seen) was formed in 1937 by designer Stella Brownie and partner William Fox.

RIGHT Model wearing an outfit made from a Vogue pattern by Pierre Balmain, 1949. By this point, a more nipped-in hourglass shape was emerging. Balmain set up on his own in 1945 and designed elegant, feminine daywear, reaching his zenith with luxurious gowns and costumes for Hollywood stars.

Blouses and sweaters

Rationing kept blouses simple and short, often in solid colors. A simple breast pocket was permitted. Yet no blouse was considered fashionable without the shoulder pad – these knife-edge bits of rubbery material were a predominant feature of the decade. Peasant blouses with gathered bodices were popular, and after the war blouses became more diaphanous, with colorful prints, deeper necklines, and bows.

For sweaters, *Vogue* declared that basic simplicity and surface decoration were the trends. Indeed, sweaters were a big fashion in the war years, partly because they were so versatile and warm. To counteract the restrictive mood, they were often highly decorated with sequins and beads, which endowed outfits with much-needed razzmatazz and glitz.

Skirts and trousers

No wider than 80 inches and with hems no deeper than two inches, the skirt epitomized the restrictions of wartime clothing. Flounces and ruffles were out, and a strict not-below-the-knee length was official. Tailored and narrow over the hips, the skirt had a casual, no-nonsense look, often with just a front and black pleat, to save material, or no pleats at all. As the decade wore on, American women were seen in fuller dirndl skirts, which twirled around as they danced to the big band sound.

After the war, skirts were longer and slimmer – although even during the war, women had been letting their hems down. In Britain, despite rationing until 1949, the female silhouette changed, and coupon clothing featured lightly gathered skirts with soft unpressed pleats and a subtle flare. These were often made in rayon and were perfect for dancing. Knife pleats came in and other skirts had discreet padding and a floating softness to the cut. As the waist grew smaller, *Vogue* featured exercises to achieve the desired shape.

Wartime occupations required practical dress, and fitted flannel trousers, especially in gray, were popular. Casual slacks were worn during the day as part of a sartorial economy drive to save on afternoon dresses.

Day-to-evening dresses

The pared-down military silhouette was echoed in the standardized dresses of the war years. Tailored and made on restricted lines, they featured shoulder pads, stitched box pleats at the front and back of the skirt, buttons to the waist, and a slim belt. They had narrow lapels with collars and cuffs sometimes in contrasting colors. As rationing took hold, designers made use of the fact that women would probably be able to afford only one dress; so jacket dresses with smooth lines were introduced. *Vogue* called them the "war-wise dress," as they were so adaptable to wartime conditions, looking smart from morning right through the evening.

Bodices were often tight-fitting, buttoned to a low waist, and with a gathered or pleated skirt. Decorative rayon dresses in pretty, colorful prints with draping and shirred fronts, sometimes with a soft crossover bodice, were worn in the daytime. Mexican prints were popular and loved for their exotic color, giving a touch of drama to the otherwise drab uniformity of the day. As material restrictions increased, sleeves were shortened and the cap sleeve was introduced, sometimes slashed to give ease of movement. Particularly popular were dolman and three-quarter-length sleeves.

The manufacture of metal zippers was severely hit by the war, and consequently the zipper-less dress was a hit. All stitching, seaming, and buttons were for use and not for decoration. In the United States, turn-up cuffs, double yokes, and sashes were banned.

After the war, a deep, rounded neckline became a popular feature and dresses had a drapier, fuller-skirted feel and extended below the knee. The waist grew smaller, and pleats were widely in evidence.

ABOVE The British Jacqmar label. A fabric manufacturer, Jacqmar was known for producing propaganda prints during the war years

OPPOSITE LEFT Air-force blue 1940s Jacqmar day suit, with military detailing at the shoulder line.

OPPOSITE RIGHT Yellow 1940s crepe dress. Note the draping at the waist and the classic '40s-style cap sleeves, here gathered to fall from the shoulder.

SIGNATURE 1940S DETAILS:

+ Fly fronts on jackets to emphasize their straight cut
+ Flap pockets on jackets
+ Bolero jackets
+ Narrow lapels on jackets and flyaway lapels on blouses and dresses
+ Dolman sleeves
+ Tiny kick pleats to soften the straight skirt
+ Crossover bodices on dresses and blouses
+ Suits piped with velvet or grosgrain
+ Pussycat bows on blouses and dresses
+ Shirring on bodices and skirts
+ Sparkling buttons on plain cardigan jackets

FAR LEFT Most daywear was in conservative colors, though many dresses and blouses were made in bright floral and naturalistic prints, as here.

LEFT Women's suit jackets were military-influenced in style, with high or rounded lapels.

Austerity Clothing

The Utility suit in Britain, the Victory suit of the United States, and "everyman" clothing in Germany were key elements of the cloth and clothing schemes that were introduced in Europe and North America during the war. The aim was to restrict style and simplify design to save material and labor. In the U.S., designers like Tina Leser and Claire McCardell (under Townley Frocks) created uncluttered, inexpensive ready-to-wear that reflected the fabric scarcities of the time.

In Britain, the Board of Trade worked with a number of leading designers to produce the kind of fashions that fitted the framework of the clothing orders. The group included Norman Hartnell, Bianca Mosca, and Hardy Amies, who designed a range of 34 Utility designs all bearing the CC41 label. The collection contained four basic items: a coat, suit, afternoon dress, and suit dress for the office. Hartnell designed some of the best-known Utility suits and dresses for Berkertexon Bond Street. Using leading designer names was a way of making prototype garments more attractive. And with their individual "signature," these items became sought after by the fashion-conscious of the decade. A Mosca dress advertised in *Vogue* in July 1942 has buttons inscribed "Austerity Bianca Mosca." Standards of manufacture were controlled, and the public demanded long-wearing, well-made clothes. Wonderful tailoring and double stitching make 1940s vintage among the best.

Siren suits

When the air-raid siren went, women reached for their Utility siren suit. An all-in-one garment, it was the original jumpsuit. It had a quick-zippered front and was not only practical but warm. Elsa Schiaparelli designed a beautiful one in silk with large slouch pockets, and Digby Morton showed zipped and hooded siren suits in tartan Viyella. Over the siren suit, people would wear the kangaroo cloak coat – so called for its large pockets.

Dollar couture

The French couture houses shut down during the war to make way for munitions, but Britain continued to promote designs and fabrics such as Harris tweed abroad to procure much-needed dollars. Designers such as Hartnell, Molyneux, and others created beautiful dramatic couture pieces that were exempt from austerity and featured the long-barred dressmaking details. There was much play of color and design in the British collections; *Vogue* wrote in 1946, "Mushroom pinks, yellows and bright greens. Floral and narrative prints on crepe and silk. A soft feminine feel with sloping shoulders, rounded hips, easy bloused fit...much hip swathing and skirts drawn back in modified bustles... raglan sleeves, softly tailored suits, draped evening gowns in embroidered chiffon and daytime dresses often with floral and narrative prints."

ABOVE The luxury export Utility label was identified by its unique circle and stroke emblem. The alternative CC41 label marked all clothes manufactured under the Civilian Clothing Order, which severely regulated the materials used.

FAR LEFT Norman Hartnell brown 1940s Utility suit. Hartnell made well-tailored suits and coats in woolens and tweeds but was most lauded for his elaborately embroidered and sequined evening gowns. Utility designs followed the square-shouldered and short-skirted fashions of the war era but adhered to strict regulations for using minimal cloth. Buttons were limited to three, and turn-back cuffs were forbidden.

LEFT Black floral 1940s Utility dress for luxury export only.

OPPOSITE Schiaparelli's air-raid jumpsuit. The garment was easy to remove and had zippered pockets for valuables, making it ideal for wearing in air-raid shelters.

Colors and Textiles

During the war years, women would walk down the street in America and Britain in outfits coordinated in the colors of the American flag and the Union Jack — red, white, and blue. Such names as air-force blue, army tan, flag red, and cadet blue all enforced the notion of patriotism and made the wearer feel that she was helping the war effort.

Drab colors were the rule in the early 1940s as dyes were diverted to help the cause. Blues, browns, greens, and black were all part of wartime understatement. Necessity became fashion. *Vogue* showed suits and dresses in soft beige, green, and gray flannel. In the magazine's famous "economy portfolio," it advised the reader how to "brighten up a brown suit with a red bolero or soften with a soft blue hat...wear your grey suit with a red tie printed blue and a dramatic red belt."

Naturalistic colors like salad and bottle green were popular, and plain rayon dresses in dark colors were given dramatic relief with the clever use of shirring and draping. Despite a uniform drabness, color did filter through in the form of exotica. Ocher yellows, terracotta reds, and clay tones came from Mexico. These were often used to liven up dresses and suits, especially those made out of black — often using blackout material; a typical example might be an ocher bolero top over a black evening dress. After the war, the color palette changed to reflect the lightness of mood. Roses and pale blues swept in, as "gray turned to gay," in the words of a British fashion writer. Shirtdresses were worn in lively colors like yellows and chartreuse, and patterns became more whimsical.

Rayon was the dominant fabric of the decade and was used from coupon to couture. Practical and economical, it was the perfect stand-in for silk and linen. It had the appearance of silk, it was noncrushable, and it did not shrink or stretch. Made in two weights, the heavier linen variety for suits and the lighter rayon crepe for dresses, it was double-faced and looked elegant enough for eveningwear, which was often made in the new Celanese-printed crepe.

Linen was another material used extensively for the war, so was used mostly for export couture rather than for everyday clothes; wonderful evening dresses and suits can be found in 1940s linen. In Britain, cotton could not be used, as it came from India, so Scottish linen replaced it and by the late 1940s linen prints were part of the move to lift people's spirits. Appliqué surface design techniques were also much in evidence. Flowered appliqué was pretty and added dimension to otherwise plain linen or rayon outfits.

Because wool was in very short supply, as it was used for uniforms and blankets for the soldiers, wool blends were introduced, along with fabrics made out of recycled wool and rayon versions of the material. Synthetic jersey was a fashionable substitute, used to create the ubiquitous jersey shift. Velveteen and corduroy became the new materials for suits and dresses. Other fabrics that were not needed for the war effort, such as net, taffeta, and faille, were used for evening dresses.

Prints and patterns

Great play was made with prints, using them cleverly with their own accent. Close bands of dots or other motifs, for instance, outlined yokes and pockets. Homey geometric designs, based on the plaids of the pioneering cowboy, were taken up in the war. Part of the frontier fashion, plaid and gingham were used to make romper suits, shirtdresses, and eveningwear. Icons of popular culture and cozy domesticity, regional scenes, and even cacti and pink thimbles made their way onto clothes and were part of the trend for narrative fashion.

RIGHT Deep-green wide-neck knit dress by Hattie Carnegie, 1943. Carnegie's designs were always youthful and chic, and her hallmarks were exquisite workmanship and fabrics. Galanos, Norell, Trigère, and McCardell all worked for her at one time or another.

BELOW Felt appliqué flowers decorate a 1940s American-made skirt.

Garden prints in salad green with cabbage roses or ferns were seen on cotton chintzes and rayons and exemplified the naturalistic theme that permeated the early part of the decade. After the war, designs became bolder and bigger and presaged the geometric abstract explosion of the 1950s. Amoebic shapes became popular, as did abstract designs of floating harps and roses in a sea of musical notes.

Patriotic and propaganda prints

Military motifs such as battleships and airplanes shoot across monotone prints, and sailors and tropical islands were other popular motifs featured in the Sears catalog of 1941. Stars and stripes, checks, and dots were the mainstay of 1940s print design. In 1942 a range of prints were made up into clothes by designer Bianca Mosca to be worn by prominent women for propaganda purposes. "Dig for Victory" and "Happy Landing" were some of the most popular mottoes. Material printed with maps and flags was made into dresses and shirts and worn with pride.

Hawaiian and ethnic influences

In California, Hawaiian prints and island motifs on sarong dresses and halter dresses were worn, especially with the growing trend for resortwear. In particular, designer Tina Leser managed to turn fabric shortages to her advantage. She cleverly fused the exotic design of island fabrics with quintessential Americana style and produced brightly patterned play clothes. She used Hawaiian, Tahitian, and Mexican fabrics, as well as prints adapted from kimono silks, and turned them into wrap skirts, sarong-style dresses, and cotton playsuits. A handwoven blanket was transformed into a strapless dress, and long, narrow pants made out of oriental fabrics were chic.

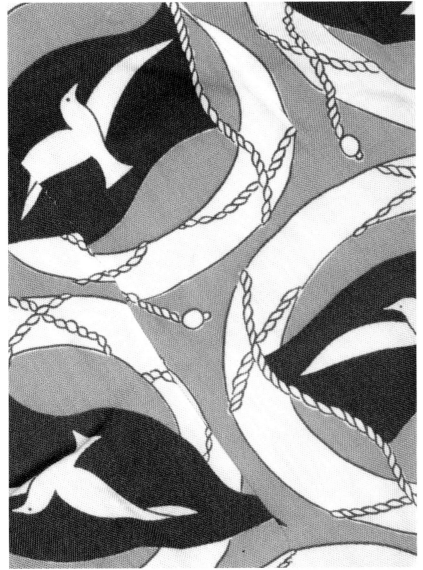

LEFT, TOP AND BOTTOM
Postwar linens featured vibrant colors and patterns, which lifted the mood after the war years. Above is a pink circle amoebic pattern on a turquoise field; below, a seagull print. Silk was rare during wartime, due to the disruption to shipping from India, and Irish linen was a useful alternative.

OPPOSITE Celanese rayon cactus-green gown, 1941. The model is standing by a barn door at dusk; her dress is indicative of the frontier fashions and natural leaf and plant motifs of the time.

The Flowering of American Style

ABOVE AND BELOW Jacket and button detail from a 1940s Lilli Ann peplum jacket. This American label, founded in 1933 by Adolph Schuman, was known for its bold colors, coats and dresses, and tailored details. Schuman developed close relationships with French and Italian textile mills after the war.

ABOVE Detail from a Fred A. Block suit, opposite. This American company was known for its fabulous 1940s jewelry, made with enamels, gold metals, clear plastics, and rhinestones.

With the occupation of Paris in 1940, France was cut off from the rest of the world, and America lost its main source of direction. Until then, department stores such as Lord & Taylor and A.T. Stewart had copied and diluted Parisian couture designs, then sold them at a cheaper price thanks to mass production. New York found itself cast adrift, and a unique challenge presented itself. Add to the mix the clothing rationing in 1942 – the War Production Board put severe restrictions on the use of wool and the amount of yardage that could be used in garments with its Regulation L-85 – and America was left to create its own style.

The Victory suit

The dominant style through to 1946 was the American Victory suit, which – while echoing the austerity lines of the British Utility suit – was far less grim. The severely cut suit was, in fact, attributed to costume designer Gilbert Adrian, who designed the austere look during the 1930s for Joan Crawford when he wanted to emphasize her authority and independence. In 1941, when he set up his ready-to-wear business, he emboldened his designs and gave women the broad-shouldered geometric suit with its three-dimensional tailoring and design detailing, which accentuated the bust and waist. Self-piping ties at the fronts of jackets replaced hard-to-come-by buttons, and sleeves were narrow. Adrian Originals suits and evening gowns were so popular that they were rationed to two per customer at his Beverly Hills store.

Ready-to-wear separates

Top-of-the-line ready-to-wear American designers such as Jo Copeland, Vera Maxwell, Norman Norell, and Claire McCardell all became household names and designed mix-and-match separates for the real woman. Unadorned and uncluttered, ready-to-wear styles avoided padding, corsetry, and built-in bras and instead followed the natural line of the body. Classic items such as the tailored shirtwaist dress made of gabardine, the drawstring-waisted dress, and the narrow synthetic jersey shift dress were easy to wear and elegant. Bright sporty plaids, checks, and stripes were often used in daywear and eveningwear and halter necks were worn with culottes and flat pumps.

The trend of peasant-inspired clothes was important during the war years. Designers used prints handwoven in places like Mexico and Hawaii. Women wore peasant skirts with blouses with signature drawstring necklines and puffed sleeves. Louella Ballerino's famous peasant dresses, with her bold prints and wide, bright stripes, are coveted vintage items.

Claire McCardell was perhaps the most influential originator of the American casual style. Forerunner of Calvin Klein, she liked simple, uncomplicated designs in

ABOVE AND RIGHT A 1940s
suit with the inside label
detail by Fred A. Block.
Block produced typically
American-styled tailored
suits in the 1940s, often
featuring studded
patterns, as here.

LEFT Steel-gray double-
breasted fitted suit by
Manhattan designer
Larry Aldrich, 1946.

LEFT Claire McCardell's
Arabian Nights trouser set
in gray rayon jersey, 1946,
shows her simple chic
styling and feminine shape.

sundresses, with the famous spaghetti straps, which
crisscrossed repeatedly to form a halter back, were
thought the height of chic, especially when worn with
the ballet pumps she introduced to the consumer.

Classic sportswear

During the war, America was forced to use its own
materials and techniques. One main inspiration was
sportswear, which had started in the 1930s on the
college campuses and the relaxed West Coast. Worn by
the stars, the look had trickled down to the department
stores. Designers showed weekend wardrobes with mix-
and-match pieces, such as jackets that could be worn
with slacks or over cardigans or predinner dresses. Wool
ribbed pullovers over white polo shirts, and crisp neat
slacks, shorts, and buttoned-down skirts were modeled
by young healthy-looking models. The lines were created
by such California manufacturers as Fay Foster, Koret,
Jantzen, and Cole of California.

Pat Premo golf dresses and Koret's topstitched
pleated skirts were all quality-made sportswear designs.
Often in two-tone plaids, they looked crisp and smart.
The Californian sundress, in cool white cotton, and
backless "sunshiners" in gingham with flutter ruffles
and edged in rickrack were worn by younger women,
and the jumper with fitted bodice and gathered waist, as
seen in the Sears catalog, was both cute and
practical. The bare-waist playsuit – with its bralike top
and brief short skirt with front buttons or side zipper
and underpanties with snug legs – was created in the
1940s and the midriff was born – not to shock but to
save on material! These were loved by Hollywood
starlets who wore them when posing for such
publications as *Life* magazine. Swimwear was glamorous
and alluring in the 1940s. Inspired by Hollywood pinups
like Betty Grable, flattering one-pieces were often made
of gold and silver Lastex. Sculpted with built-in boning
and elasticized nylon, and featuring shirring and draping
used in eveningwear, these flattering items clung in
the right places and minimized the flaws of the
wayward female figure. Pareus, pajama pants, pirate
shorts, and wrap skirts were all sold to coordinate with
and, more crucially, to cover up the new brief styles.

Hollywood glamour

Hollywood lost its glamour in the 1940s and was not
exempt from L-85 regulations. Gritty realism films set
an example by showing actresses like Bette Davis and
Joan Crawford in suits, skirts, sweaters, and slacks. The
Hollywood western gave America frontier fashion –
fringe on jackets and shirts and denim detailing were
commonplace. Frontier pants with front paneling and
topstitching were popular with stylish women and fitted
in with their growing independence. Blue jeans, made
sexy in the 1950s by a young Marilyn Monroe, were
specially cut for the feminine figure, with side
openings at the cuff, as these were more ladylike.

unsophisticated fabrics, such as chambray, cotton jersey,
denim, and mattress ticking. She incorporated the
functionality of sportswear and experimented with
pattern and cut to create great pantsuits with graph-
paper checks (a McCardell trademark) and long shorts in
wool jersey with streamlined hooded sweaters. When her
monastic dress was brought out, *Vogue* heralded it a
triumph. Loosely fitted and shaped like a voluminous
tent, it created a soft shape when belted. Women loved
her popover dress, a simple wrapover design often
with a dramatic belt, and they lined up to buy her play
clothes in denim with white topstitching. Finally, her

OPPOSITE Summer dresses
with the trademark graph-
paper check by Claire
McCardell, 1946. Her midriff-
baring designs heralded a
new relaxed style, which was
made for leisure activities.
She used fabrics such as
jersey, denim, and other
cottons to produce her
sportswear-influenced
classics.

Eveningwear

Despite the wartime devastation, civilization reasserted itself during the evening. Extensive drapery and dazzle created the much-needed illusion of glamour and was in stark contrast to prosaic daywear. Dinner suits were popular and often consisted of long, plain dresses that could be worn with or without sparkly jackets. Shorter evening dresses with draped bodices and low-slung sarong skirts were worn to save materials, yet still managed to look sophisticated. By mid-decade the little black cocktail dress was considered a vital part of any woman's wardrobe.

Sequins were not rationed and seemed to be sewn on everything, long or short. Jeweled bodices and glass starring provided welcome sparkle on otherwise plain dresses, and jeweled capes were thrown over to glitter in the dark. Evening dresses often had to be made out of undyed material (called "greige goods").

The column shift dress

The slim body-conscious lines that were set in the 1930s were followed in the 1940s, and the tubular shift evening dress, inspired by Greek statuary, was much in evidence. In a bid to save material, this style was used in many guises, from dinner suits to opulent gowns. Adrian's columnar evening gowns, embroidered with gold beads and Greek bands, circa 1945, is one such example. Dresses based on the toga and the pleated chiton, in rayon crepe, were all features of the decade.

While silk had been the preferred choice in the 1930s, now that other fabrics had to be used, rayon became a favorite for evening. Having a silk-like quality, while being much cheaper and unrationed, rayon was draped and shirred to form fluid dresses that maintained that 1930s "poured in" look. Side-draped, side-buttoned simple dresses made out of black rayon were particularly popular. Shirred bodices and front-bodice drapery are characteristic of the period. Short bolero jackets were worn over sheath dresses with draped crossover bodices in two different colors.

Capes and cutaway jackets made out of taffeta and net covered up the plain dresses and were part of the wartime trend of mixing and matching to create more outfits. The strapless evening gown showed off the female sloping shoulder line and was much in evidence − it saved material and was elegant to boot.

LEFT Star sequin-studded midnight-blue rayon-and-net evening dress and cape by Hattie Carnegie, 1945. Sequins were much used, as there were no wartime restrictions on them.

Export couture gowns

While most British women made do with Utility garments, couture evening gowns were exuberant and luxurious. Reserved for export, they escaped austerity rules, and designers indulged their fantasies in these creations, such as beautiful taffeta shawls over molded tubes of satin or jersey and black velvet bodices with plunging necklines. Hip drapery caught in bustles added to the flamboyant feel of such gowns, especially when topped off with wildly bouffant sleeves. Eveningwear was often sculpted and seemed to envelop the wearer.

The Molyneux export collections are particularly noteworthy and featured beautiful floor-length gowns with complicated embroidery and luxury fabrics. The designer's black full-length gown in slipper satin with pink bertha and hem and weighted with roses had dropped shoulders and oodles of fabric.

Elsa Schiaparelli's love of color, high drama, and sartorial frivolity all coincided in her close-fitting mermaid dresses: These flared at the bottom and were accompanied by hip-length capes in gaudy colors with her signature fantasy embroidery. Her bustle dresses appeared in many fabrics in 1939, and her exuberant evening gowns are coveted items. In 1941 Schiaparelli left for New York, where she remained until the war was over. Schiaparelli's house remained open throughout the war and produced collections, although they were not created by the designer herself. Her early wartime designs were made before she departed for America.

Americana and American designers

New York was a haven for couture and glamour. The American halfway-hem ballet skirts in such fabrics as mousseline, with tiny waists and full skirts, presaged the New Look and were not available in Europe. Hattie Carnegie's little black cocktail dress was worn by women all over the country.

In the United States, materials like gingham and other cottons were being used in evening dresses. Gilbert Adrian employed gingham and Pennsylvania Dutch motifs in his Dolley Madison ballgowns, made in organdy and patterned with patchwork-quilt designs. Claire McCardell's halter-neck evening dresses made out of gingham looked simple and unpretentious. Gingham was also used frequently by Anglo-American Charles James, head of costume at MGM, from 1928 to 1941, who famously used gingham to dress Judy Garland as Dorothy in *The Wizard of Oz* (1939); later, he adapted this weave pattern for checked wool suits.

James elevated dressmaking into an art form. His ballgowns are sartorial sculptures with asymmetrical shapes, which were made in such unforgiving fabrics as velvet, heavy satin, and faille. His full, intricately shaped skirts over understructures were classically elegant. He disliked printed fabric and would create dresses using several different types of material all in the same color range. His color combinations were unusual – such as

orange and rose, or black and eggplant. His sculptural approach to eveningwear is reflected in a series of gowns he made during the 1940s that became known as "Charlies." A dressmaker of consummate skill, he got a Coty American Fashion Critics Award for his "magical use of color and artistic mastery of drapery."

Other noted couturiers of the period include the Russian-born American Valentina Sanina, who favored couture clothes that looked effortless and understated and operated a small house known as Valentina Gowns. Known for her floor-gracing silk jersey gowns and her bolero evening creations, Valentina was a meticulous designer with an eye for the dramatic. Norman Norell's evening gowns were striking in their simplicity, and he favored a revealing round neckline that he would offset with jeweled buttons or pussycat bows. His prolific use of sequins and beads – often covering entire garments – is testament to his admitted love of the 1920s, as was his use of the straight up-and-down silhouette. Jo Copeland's grand evening gowns are a collector's dream. She worked with pure silk, rayon, and wool and loved asymmetrical cascading ruffles, trumpet-flaring skirts, and wide side draperies.

OPPOSITE Fuchsia ballgown in concentrically flaring taffeta; in the background is a lead-colored faille gown with underskirt of gunmetal satin; both by Charles James, 1946. James was a master of the sculptural cut that spiraled around the body.

BELOW Vera Zorina wearing a white crepe gown and Valentina Sanina wearing a black crepe dress, 1940, in Valentina's Paris shop. Valentina designs were timeless and elegant.

FAR LEFT AND LEFT Black 1940s evening gown and jacket with coral-encrusted beadwork at the neckline and jacket collar. The jacket is fastened with a visible zipper. The avant-garde use of gold sequins encased in gold mesh combined with coral is a technique very similar to that used by Elsa Schiaparelli.

Surface decoration on eveningwear

The early years of the 1940s were characterized by an ornate look that was left over from the extravagant 1930s. As the wartime restrictions bit hard, surface decoration was replaced by clever shirring, tucking, and appliqué. Beaded dresses were fashionable throughout the decade, and sequins were the queen of the evening, as these were not restricted by the wartime effort; all-over beading is a characteristic of '40s eveningwear. Gold palettes and black sequins livened up dresses, and bead embroidery, often in the shape of jewelery, gave glamour to the pared-down styles. Postwar luxury was a welcome respite and the Paris collections featured full-blown evening gowns in taffeta and satin with lace trims and even silver fox on the hems of capes and coats.

Postwar eveningwear

After the war, eveningwear took on a softer, more feminine feel. The postwar silhouette with its rounded shoulders and gathered skirts was reiterated in the evening gowns that showed a much tinier waist and more flounce. Romantic satin gowns of rayon net flared below a slim waistline, and showed bows, flounces, and low-cut necklines with ruching and puffed sleeves. These elements were influenced by the Southern belle, glamorized in films like *Jezebel* (1938) and *Gone with the Wind* (1939).

This romantic femininity that harked back to the prewar period was ironically to appear in a flurry of net taffeta in 1947, when Christian Dior's New Look burst on the scene. His evening dresses were so whale-boned and petticoated that they could stand unaided. The tiny waistline was achieved only by wearing a *guêpière* – a type of corset – and the yards of tulle made women look like meringues. The sloping shoulders and deep plunging neckline showed off the rounded female body once again, and the wartime silhouette had gone for good.

DECORATIVE ELEMENTS OF THE 1940S:

* Jet, bugle, and glass beadwork and bead-embroidered waistbands
* Sparkling and covered buttons used as decorative elements in themselves
* Sequins and beads that simulated jewelery
* Appliqué and piqué appliqué
* Grecian bands of gold and silver embroidery
* Satin roses on bodice fronts and hems weighted with roses
* Double-puffed peplums and giant back bows made of taffeta and silk
* Pleated lace collars and demure eyelet ruffles
* Fur pom-poms on dinner-jacket sleeves
* Silk and moiré sashes on tulle gowns
* Laced V-necked bodices

RIGHT Mother-of-pearl beadwork adorning the front of an early-1940s Molyneux bolero evening jacket. This piece was probably created while the French couture houses were still in full operation – prior to 1942.

RIGHT Pink velvet 1940s evening jacket with black frogging and beads by Stassner.

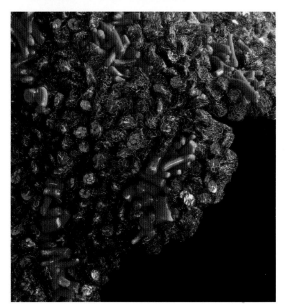

RIGHT Detail of the coral and gold sequins encased in mesh on the evening gown pictured opposite.

▼ Slacks

All styles of slacks, especially pioneer pants, became popular as women got used to wearing trousers at work. Here, actress Lilli Palmer is shown in 1946 wearing her man-tailored gray gabardine slacks, along with a beige suede jacket.

▶ Sequins and beads

Not rationed by the war, sequins were sewn on dresses, jackets, and shawls to add sparkle to daywear and eveningwear. This 1945 white crepe gown, covered with bugle beads and featuring dolman sleeves, is by New York costume designer Kiviette.

Utility or Victory suit

Clothing by law. Designed along tailored lines in military-style boxy jacket and narrow short skirt, they were most often made in blue, black, and brown.

Key looks of the decade
1940s

▶ Trench coats

Military styling was evident in jackets and coats during the war years; here, a red wool belted trench coat, lined in black rabbit, is by Traina-Norell, 1943. Bell-shaped coats with large collars were also popular.

▲ Gingham

A favorite American fabric. Shirtdresses and jumpers all had a fresh new look in gingham, which became popular during the war years. This 1947 blue gingham dress is worn with a red gingham scarf and red kid shoes.

Couture eveningwear
Structured couture gowns in satin featured elaborate detailing and were made in unforgiving fabrics such as velvet and heavy satin and faille. Classically inspired sheath dresses with soft draping or pleating were made in rayon crepe and greige goods.

Monastic dress
Loosely fitted and shaped like a voluminous tent, the dress was given a soft shape when belted.

Peasant dress
Exotic handwoven printed skirts and off-the-shoulder blouses with drawstring necklines and puffed sleeves were popular, partly due to the success of the Brazilian bombshell Carmen Miranda.

▶Bolero jacket
Short and emphasizing the waist, with padded shoulders, the bolero was often worn over strapless evening dresses. Here a navy bolero is worn with a white blouse and red skirt – classic patriotic colors – in 1942.

Jersey shift dress
Simple and elegant, the shift was a shortish unstructured design in synthetic jersey, which was made popular by New York designers such as Norman Norell.

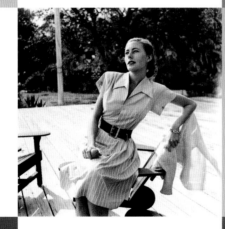

▲Sportswear and beach
Summer dresses and midriff-baring tops with matching shorts were influenced by outdoor athletics, as in this 1946 day dress by Claire McCardell.

Rayon print dress
Pretty for daytime wear in the new crease-resistant rayon fabric, dresses exhibited colorful prints, often with shirring and draping on the bodice or waist.

1950s

The 1950s kicked off with a feeling of hope and euphoria following the conclusion of the Second World War and the generally rapturous applause that had greeted Dior's New Look in 1947. In the United States, rationing and wartime scarcities were distant memories, and consumer goods were becoming plentiful. In Britain, where rationing would drag on until 1954, the outlook was more subdued, although in 1951, the government, promising to "Make Britain Great Again," organized a cultural exhibition, the Festival of Britain, on the South Bank of the Thames in a bid to raise morale. In the fashion industry, optimism prevailed. After years of hardship and drudgery, when women had worn sexless, utilitarian work garments (and when there were fewer men around to impress), there was an understandable desire to dress up in luxurious, feminine clothes. The sheer extravagance of Dior's New Look seemed to point to a future of confidence and prosperity — something that everyone aspired to. Dior's designs were to dominate, but not everyone was thrilled; for some, Dior seemed out of tune with postwar Europe and a symbol of luxury, extravagance — some of his skirts required 20 yards of material — and privilege that many hoped the war had destroyed. Times had definitely changed. For all the hardships and tragedies that women had dealt with during the war, it had in fact been a time of liberation and equality. Thousands of young women had gone to work in factories and in the armed forces. The idea that fashion now intended them to revert to a romantic notion of femininity, with a padded bosom and nipped-in waist, was something many were not prepared for.

Fit or Flounce Silhouettes

PAGE 84 Model wearing a Balenciaga evening dress and wrap with a black hat, and diamonds by Van Cleef & Arpels, 1952. Balenciaga was noted for his refined elegance; his gigantic flounces and sculptural cutting created a frame for the body.

BELOW Taffeta shantung dresses in the New Look shape, 1951. Coordinating hats and gloves were very much part of the polished look of the period.

The 1950s were the last decade when Paris still dominated worldwide fashion. Dior was unstoppable, and he remained influential until his death in 1957; alongside him were other great designers determined to succeed. Cristóbal Balenciaga, Jacques Fath, and Hubert de Givenchy were all leading names of the era. But the clock was ticking, and as the decade unfolded, there were signs that the elitism of haute couture was starting to lose its dominance. The decade was a transitional one that moved from the austerity of the 1940s to the prosperity of the 1960s. In fact, the dividing line was becoming clearer by 1956, with the increasing influence of the teenage youth culture in the United States and the identification of the young as a separate consumer group.

The decade will be remembered mainly for two contrasting silhouettes, although there were myriad alternative shapes (not all of which were very successful) that flourished briefly and then disappeared. The great full skirt that swirled and sashayed and the slim pencil tubular skirt that fell to below the knee were quintessential silhouettes, and both placed great emphasis on the narrowness of the waist. After the miserable war years, women were eager to embrace femininity. Strategic padding and structured underwear did much to improve a less-than-perfect body, so that Dior's extreme silhouette of

1951/52 – Ligne Longue

1952 – Ligne Sinueuse

1952/53 – Ligne

ne Tulipe

1953/54 – Ligne Vivante

1954 – Ligne Muguet

1954/55 – Ligne H

1955 – Ligne A

1955/56 – Ligne Y

1956 – Ligne Flèche

nipped-in waist and swirling mid-calf skirt could look fabulous on everyone. The nylon all-in-one corselet gave a waspish waist, pulled in the hips, and shunted the breasts upward and outward to give a perfect hourglass figure, as seen in Anita Ekberg in Fellini's *La Dolce Vita* (1960). Fashion was still dictating rigid and uncomfortable dress codes, and women continued to fall into line, as they wanted to appear alluring and sophisticated.

Women everywhere fell in love with the glamorous clothes of the time, chronicled as the "fashion-conscious '50s." An elegant appearance required the correct accessories, and smart women were still expected to wear hats, gloves, and matching shoes and handbag to be considered well dressed. Although functionality and simplicity were increasingly prevalent in daywear (easy separates and sporty slacks reflected an increased interest in athletics), eveningwear was dramatically showstopping, with long gloves, high heels, and drop earrings essential to complete the look. Hair was worn high on the head, in the beehive style, or cut short to the face in a gamine Jean Seberg crop.

Dior's hourglass figure was not the only silhouette of the decade, though, and he himself experimented with many other shapes; almost every Dior collection saw the introduction of a new silhouette – the Princess line, the A-line, the H-line, and the S-line all followed each other in quick succession. Dior's invention of the A-line was simply a dress that fell from fitted shoulders outward toward the hem and used stiffened fabric to create the shape. The A-line and the H-line were offering women even more choice, and another set of vastly contrasting shapes was hailed as the latest look.

The waistline started to fluctuate, changes in length and line came quickly, and women were expected to keep up with many innovative directions. Skirts ranged from voluminous fullness through neat tailored pleats to snug slim-line pencils. The Sack, Princess, Tulip, and Trapeze lines were all to come and go before the end of the decade, as designers seemed to waver between very structured clothes, which could almost support themselves, and clothes that were much more fluid and relied on the female body to provide form and shape.

ABOVE Almost every Christian Dior collection of the decade featured a new silhouette, though all kept a narrow waist and a below-knee hemline.

RIGHT Mexican 1950s circle skirt. Note the ornate and colorful print and sequin detailing, popular in peasant-style circle skirts of the 1950s. Appliqué, rickrack, screenprinting, sequins, and glitter, as well as ethnic scenes, dominated, often featuring cowboy and western scenes and other Americana prints.

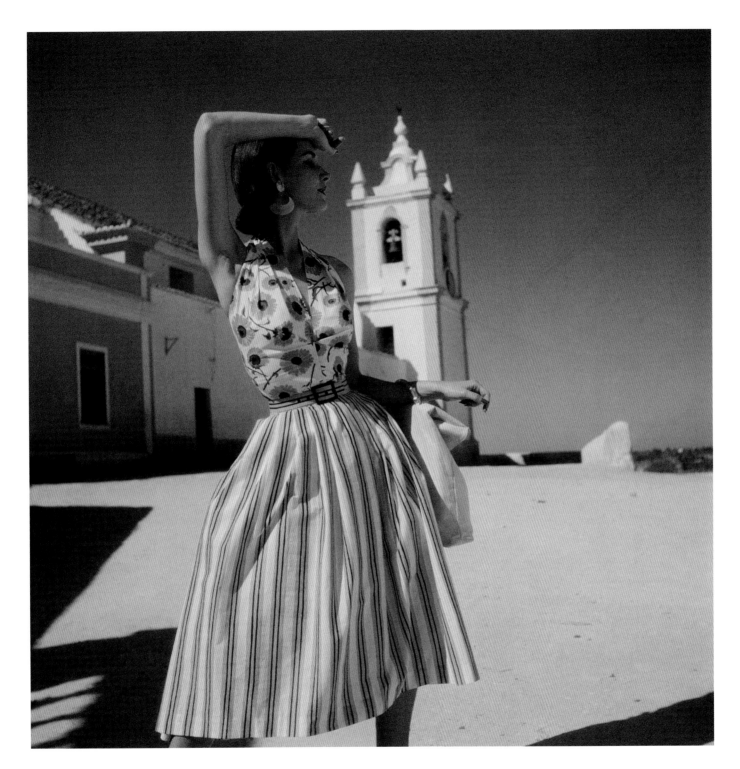

A more relaxed attitude

Other designers began to nurture the lifestyle changes that were taking place around the globe and encouraged women to develop a more relaxed attitude to clothing, with designs that were less formal and allowed more freedom of movement.

A master of undulating line, Jacques Fath came to prominence in the postwar period, with a less structured approach than Cristóbal Balenciaga or Christian Dior. The first Frenchman to design for the American ready-to-wear market, under Joseph Halpert, Fath catered to high

ABOVE Floral halter-neck top and striped skirt by Texan Tom Brigance, 1952. Brigance designed for Lord & Taylor and others before starting his own label in 1949. Noted for casual wear, he claimed his ethos was to make clothes "appropriate for the American woman's mode of living."

ABOVE AND RIGHT Dogstooth 1950s suit by Charles Worth, in a classic fitted shape. The house of Worth was known for innovative sleeve variations and trimmings, as seen here in the unusual three-quarter pleated sleeve and, above, the pleating detailing in the pocket.

society and the Hollywood set with his showy elegance and asymmetrical necklines, which drew attention to the breasts. Daring to use such vibrant color combinations as green and blue, his daywear and eveningwear were also noted for their diagonal lines and panels, which were designed to enhance the female form. He set up his own ready-to-wear line in Paris just before his tragic early death in 1954 from leukemia.

Hubert de Givenchy, another leading name, had studied with Jacques Fath in the 1940s and then left to set up his own couture house in 1952. He became known for structured, minimalist clothing and was the first to design a collection of separates. Givenchy went on to create the Sack dress and the funnel-collared coat. His success in designing beautiful, understated clothes for Audrey Hepburn in the movie *Sabrina* in 1954 led to a collaboration between the actress and the house of Givenchy that lasted for more than 40 years. In 1957 Givenchy started the trend for straighter, shiftlike dresses that had no waist at all by inventing his Sack dress. It was almost formless in shape, and although women could still look elegant by the addition of jewelry or a hat, it was a revolutionary breakthrough, as it freed them from the restrictive clothing to which they had become accustomed. The Sack was to have lasting influence, as it became the springboard for Mary Quant's early tunic dresses, which launched her meteoric rise from the tail end of the 1950s into the explosive 1960s.

Crossovers from couture to ready-to-wear

Ranging from casual wear to formal evening gowns, ready-to-wear took off after the war. Many designers never revealed their full names on the garment labels, instead collaborating with others. In Britain the Irish-born Digby Morton, though prominent in the Utility schemes of the 1940s (see pages 66–7), was a postwar ready-to-wear designer who found favor in the American market. Under the name Reldan-Digby Morton, he introduced ready-made clothes to the British public that happened to have a couture appeal, as well as a collection of separates, which were successful in both the United States and Britain. For his wearable tailoring, Morton used traditional fabrics, but in less conventional colorways. His clever cutting and stitching lines gave new life to the traditional tweed suit.

Another Irish-born designer and traditionalist in the use of Irish wools and tweeds who found success

OPPOSITE Tailored ready-to-wear suits, 1953. The narrow fitted silhouette made the hips look slim and the legs longer.

The burgeoning youth market

By mid-decade, all the major French fashion houses had started to diversify. Product lines such as shoes, jewelry, leather goods, and, of course, perfume were being licensed around the world, and small boutiques full of *prêt-à-porter* (ready-to-wear) collections were appearing in major cities. Existing manufacturing businesses like Maison Weill and Lempereur (the first to use the young Brigitte Bardot to model its range) started to look for talented young designers to create their own style of clothes for the burgeoning youth market. Up-and-coming designers like Daniel Hechter, Emmanuelle Khanh, and Jean Charles de Castelbajac were contracted to such companies as Lempereur and Pierre D'Alby before finding success under their own names, and a young Karl Lagerfeld designed for the prêt-à-porter label Chloé with great success.

Shapewise, the 1950s continued to be a decade of contrasts. The sheath dress and empire-line dress relied on superb cutting skills to construct a fitted garment that followed the contours of the body with invisible seaming and darts. Completely opposing this refined line, other fashion in the decade was known for volume, and designers played with billowing shapes in the form of tulip skirts, balloon-type jackets, huge cocooning capes, and generously cut swing coats, sometimes held in place with a half-belt to control the fluidity.

When Christian Dior died suddenly at the age of 52 in 1957, a youthful Yves Saint Laurent was waiting in the wings to take on his mantle. His first collection for Dior in 1958 was a huge success with a refined Trapeze line, which fell from narrow shoulders to a wider hemline that just covered the knees, but there was a huge outcry at his next collection, which introduced a hobble-type skirt, and his time at the house was short-lived. Designers were becoming increasingly in tune with the changes in society and the shift toward a younger client. The image of Bardot, long-haired and barefoot in a cute cotton gingham dress, encapsulated the carefree spirit of the times, which was to dominate the next 10 years.

ABOVE: Model wearing Digby Morton's camel-hair-and-wool suit with a felt cloche by Knox, pictured in front of a Rolls-Royce, circa 1953.

on both sides of the Atlantic was Sybil Connolly. Inspired by Givenchy to make clothing that was elegant but comfortable, she worked luxury into poplin, tweed, lace, and linen, with designs influenced by Irish country pursuits and Arts and Crafts – riding habits, hooded cloaks, and shawls.

Jacques Heim created diffusion lines, Heim Actualité and Heim Jeunes Filles, in 1950, extending into ready-to-wear and specifically catering to America's need for sportswear. By the end of the decade, Jean Louis Henri Bousquet at Cacharel, with Emmanuelle Khanh, had created a ready-to-wear company image that was very French, young, and sporty. Liberty of London, meanwhile, was nurturing the talents of Jean Muir.

SIGNATURE 1950S ELEMENTS:

* Twinsets and heavily ornate beaded cardigans
* Bell-shaped coats
* Slim pencil skirts
* Boxy collarless jackets
* Strapless gowns
* Covered buttons
* Circular skirts
* Half belts
* Slacks with foot loops
* Oversized collars

LEFT AND ABOVE Front and
back views of a 1950s blue
plaid suit by Digby Morton,
an example of using a
traditional pattern in a more
elegant fabric. Note the
front panel to the skirt, the
back pleat, and the vent on
the jacket to emphasize the
waist, and the unusual
square buttons.

Cristóbal Balenciaga and Coco Chanel

Some had criticized Dior's boned bodices as backward-looking, and by 1952 Spanish-born Cristóbal Balenciaga, a master of cutting, had started to release the body by eliminating the waistline and broadening the shoulders, cutting a looser, less structured jacket to a new midi length, which fell across the hipbones. Without huge fanfare he created clothes suitable for modern living, endlessly refining to make them efficient and elegant. He perfected the semifitted suit, called the H- or I-line, which became synonymous with the decade: a long straight jacket worn over a slim pencil skirt cut to just below the knee, very chic and modern-looking when compared with previous shapes. Regarded as a sculptor among designers, Balenciaga created collarless blouses, as well as balloon-tunic sack and chemise dresses. His expertise lay in the detail of his cut, collars, and sleeves, which always looked perfectly formfitting in every situation. Known as one of the foremost designers of the decade, Balenciaga also introduced "semifit" dresses with soft, round shoulders.

Coco Chanel too had vocally criticized Dior's restrictive shape as stifling for women, and at the age of 70, after 14 years in retirement, she relaunched in 1954 with a collection of boxy, collarless jackets, with slightly flared skirts made from soft jersey fabrics. The style was perfect to copy for mass production, providing thousands of "ordinary" women with a Parisian original design at an affordable, ready-to-wear price tag, courtesy of department stores nationwide. Chanel was scathing about Dior's "upholstered" clothing and offered an alternative silhouette that was clearly feminine but much less restrictive and absolutely veered away from the boned, nipped-in look. Her classic, iconic suits consisted of a cardigan-style collarless and almost box-shaped jacket that fell open to the waist, worn over a slim skirt and decorated with trademark gilt buttons, girlish bows, and contrasting braid. It was a style that was easy to wear and was made in luxury tweeds with a contrast silk lining; it became immensely desirable for women of all ages and remains so to the present day.

OPPOSITE A poppy-red linen Balenciaga suit with a fitted front and a loose back line, accessorized with a matching hat and white gloves, 1952.

RIGHT Red tweed Chanel suit 1954–5. Cut loose and boxy, with the classic front patch pockets, the suit was made for movement.

LEFT Chanel's classic braided trim around the cardigan-style jacket became a trademark of her tailored suits.

Coats and Jackets

The 1950s saw great diversity in the styles of jackets and coats available. Dior, Fath, Balenciaga, and other couturiers experimented with less formal styles and a move away from fur. There were practical considerations too; because so many of the decade's dresses and blouses were sleeveless, there was a greater need for cardigans, jackets, and coats to keep the arms warm when the temperature dropped and to coordinate the look.

A shape that was popular from the start of the decade was a wide triangular coat, commonly called a tent or duster coat. Based loosely on Jacques Fath's swing coat of the 1940s, it was single-breasted, with wide, square armholes. It sat easily over a voluminous silhouette and was worn over cocktail sheath dresses and full-skirted eveningwear for much of the decade. Design details such as Peter Pan collars and buttonless versions with extravagant shawl collars – known as clutch coats because

BELOW AND RIGHT A 1950s jacket and inside collar label by Maria-Louise Bruyère, a French designer popular in the 1940s and 1950s. The jacket may have originally been part of a suit, or worn with a contrasting skirt.

RIGHT AND BELOW RIGHT The bow motif around the rounded collar is repeated on the buttons, creating a very feminine-style jacket.

they had to be held together by hand – were all variations on the same theme. Coats often had a contrasting lining. Popular fabrics included camel hair, wool velour, melton cloth, tweed, and velvet. Fur was reduced to trims, and beaver, lamb, astrakhan, and mink were used.

In Paris there was a definite trend toward tunic coats and flared three-quarter coats. The designer Nina Ricci, who became established in the 1930s but was still a prestigious couturier until the mid-1950s, excelled in making garments that flattered the wearer. Her hip-length boxy jackets are a perfect example of clever cutting that allows maximum freedom and ease, while her coats provided the popular bell-shaped line, which sat easily over full skirts. The soft fluid cut was her trademark and an example of Ricci's underlying design philosophy: to make women ultrafeminine and beautiful. The very loose topcoat, which covered all shapes of clothing, was also popular until the end of the decade when shapes started to change dramatically, and billowing shapes gave way to minimalist geometric pieces.

BELOW One or two buttons were all that was required over the fashionable coat. Here, a mother-of-pearl button typifies the oversized details of the time.

RIGHT Rose-print 1950s coat by Nina Ricci. The Peter Pan collar and soft gathers falling from the shoulder line into a voluminous bell shape were perfect over full-skirted dresses.

ABOVE Nina Ricci label from the inside collar of the 1950s coat, left.

Christian Dior and the Corolla Line

ABOVE AND RIGHT Sapphire silk taffeta dress, with buttoned pleated bodice, by Dior, 1952. Dior, who wanted to be an architect but became a fashion designer, said, "I created flower women with gentle shoulders and generous bosoms, with tiny waists like stems and skirts belling out like petals." His 1947 New Look hourglass silhouette harked back to the ultra-feminine belle époque ideal of voluminous long skirts and tiny, cinched-in waists, and set the prevailing shape for the 1950s.

OPPOSITE Models posing in one of the last Christian Dior collections, 1957. Note the variety of Dior lines on show, and the move from the hourglass to less restrictive forms.

In February 1947 a shy and balding designer from the provinces presented his first collection under his own name; few could have foreseen that a single show, heavily focused on one unfamiliar silhouette, would have such an impact around the world. Like all great designers, Christian Dior had the ability to capture the mood of the time; he recognized women's yearning for a return to femininity after the Second World War and presented a show in which the models looked quite unlike anything that had gone before. He called the collection *Ligne Corolle*, the "Corolla line," and it was his ambition to make women look like flowers. Charming and ladylike in expensive and glamorous fabrics, his feminine ideal had rounded shoulders, a fully formed bosom, and a tiny waist sitting on top of an enormous full skirt, which fell to about 12 inches from the floor, and wore sheer stockings and high-heeled pointed-toe shoes. This was an astonishing innovation after 13 years of women wearing square-shouldered Schiaparelli-style suits, and Carmel Snow, the editor of *Harper's Bazaar*, dubbed the elegant shape the New Look. In a single collection, Dior's reputation as one of the most important couturiers in the world was assured. The look was at once an international success, and it inspired every fashion house to produce a similar line.

Having trained originally in 1938 with Robert Piguet (where he worked alongside Pierre Balmain) and then at the much larger house of Lucien Lelong until 1946, Dior was acknowledged as an expert cutter who employed complicated dressmaking skills to achieve his finished look. From 1950, new ideas came thick and fast. It was not only the haute couture collections that established Dior's name on a global scale. He was the first designer to license a whole range of products that introduced his label to a new type of consumer. Dior was imaginative and enjoyed playing with proportions, although his clothes were always elegant and in the very best fabrics; each couture presentation had a new theme. In 1953 he presented the Tulip collection, which featured an abundance of floral patterns and colors to stunning effect; 1955 had the A-line, a trianglular shape that widened from the shoulders to a dropped waistline and then a voluminous skirt that stuck out, pleated and stiffened. Later that year came the H-line, a long, slim jacket that fell to the knee, worn over an even slimmer skirt cut a few inches longer.

Dior favored fine-quality men's suiting fabrics in graphic black-and-white check and pinstripe for most of his tailored pieces, and expensive velvet, satin, and taffeta for eveningwear. The Y silhouette was created from an oversized V-shaped collar, cut out over the shoulders, or a large stole that was draped around the shoulder line, over a very slim sheath-type body.

From 1947 to 1957 Christian Dior presented his own version of elegance, but his clothes were ruthlessly demanding, and women were expected to suffer in pursuit of old-fashioned glamour. For his final collection in 1957, the designer had at last moved attention away from the waist, and his new line appeared to be favoring a more relaxed, unstructured shape based around a simple chemise (a refinement of Givenchy's Sack dress, see page 111) with a stand-up collar and patch pockets.

His death cut short a dazzling career that had single-handedly reestablished Paris as the undisputed fashion capital of the world and had seen him dress the most celebrated women of the time, including Queen Elizabeth II and Princess Margaret, Marlene Dietrich, and Princess Grace of Monaco. When he died, there were Christian Dior boutiques in 24 countries, and his company employed more than a thousand people. Today, 50 years after his death, John Galliano is head of design at Christian Dior, and the label, which is still considered to be one of the most prestigious, has gone from strength to strength. It is even now synonymous with elegance, luxury, and innovation. Original Christian Dior pieces are hard to come by except in specialist vintage shops, where they often sell for many times the amount they would have in the 1950s. Because Dior's clothes were made in the highest-quality fabrics and by superb technicians, they can still be found in good condition.

LEFT A green satin two-piece by Christian Dior, circa 1953. The off-the-shoulder bodice with bow detail has complex internal corsetry to accentuate the waist. Many of Dior's dresses had the trademark narrow belt, as shown opposite.

SIGNATURE DIOR ELEMENTS:

- Fitted jackets with peplum at the waist
- Coolie hats
- Very full skirts
- A-line coats, flared out to below the hip
- Pleated A-line skirts, stiffened to hold their own shape
- Trapeze coats with a collarless boatneck
- Deep-cut V-neck, with very wide shoulders
- Hobble skirts, cut very long and narrow with a back split
- Strapless self-supporting evening gowns with a fitted bodice and full skirt

OPPOSITE Christian Dior's clothes made women look decorative and feminine. Here, a model wears a rose chiffon gathered bodice and black tulip-pleat skirt, with pillbox hat and wrap jacket, all by Dior, with a Louis XIV pin, 1952.

American Style

Before the war, America had bowed to Parisian superiority on the fashion front, but the war proved to be an enormous catalyst to its own fashion industry, which was not prepared to put its own manufacturing businesses on hold for five years. The United States was forced to look to its own designers – Norman Norell, Hattie Carnegie, and Mainbocher (an American living in Paris) – who went on to become leading names at the top end of the business, as well as designers like Claire McCardell, who led a thriving ready-to-wear trade.

There were other changes too that were responsible for the breakdown of Parisian-led couture. Technological advancements in the textile industry and manufacturing processes had increased during the war, and throughout the 1950s people started to embrace change and look for new ideas in every area of life. Better living accommodations, improved communication, and the expansion of commercial air travel all helped to further these aims and were a reflection of the social changes taking place across the world.

The early 1950s saw the birth of the modern fashion industry as we now know it. Manufacturers realized that there was a huge demand from "ordinary" women for high fashion without the restrictive costs. In Manhattan's Seventh Avenue (as the garment district is known), a deal was arranged with the couture houses in Europe to buy the rights for original designer clothes and to copy them precisely, stitch for stitch. Women were now able to buy good-quality, design-led garments from department stores, and this opened the floodgates for other entrepreneurs to step in and break the stranglehold that Paris had held over the fashion world. With this growing ready-to-wear market, it was becoming possible for women to choose clothes that were influenced by Paris but related more to their own real lives, for which they required clothes based on practicality and ease.

Edith Head and the motion-picture influence

Although Edith Head had no formal design education, her career as Hollywood's most famous costume designer, working under contract for all the major studios and dressing the biggest film stars of the day, spanned more than 60 years, with some of her best work achieved during the 1950s.

Starting out as an assistant at Paramount Pictures in 1927, she was made head of design in 1938 and was responsible for dressing the really glamorous stars of the day, such as Mae West, Ginger Rogers, and, later, Grace Kelly and Elizabeth Taylor. Although Head did not consider herself a couturier, she became a great American tastemaker, known for designing beautiful and flattering clothes the moviegoing public wanted to copy. In *Sunset Boulevard* (1950), her clothes for the aging silent film star Norma Desmond (Gloria Swanson)

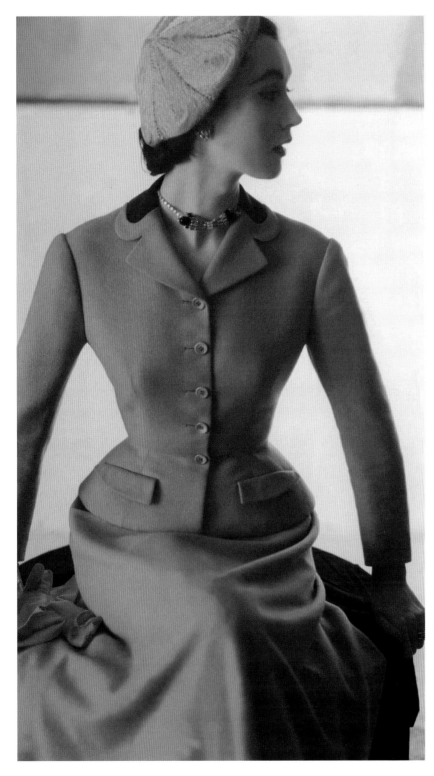

brilliantly captured a bygone era. Although she dressed Audrey Hepburn in some beautifully tailored pieces for *Roman Holiday* (1953), it was Hubert de Givenchy who designed most of Hepburn's wardrobe for *Sabrina* (1954), even though Head collected the Academy Award that year for best costume design for the film. As Head's reputation grew outside Hollywood, the studio publicity department ensured that the name Edith Head became synonymous with homegrown American fashion. As a designer she was extremely versatile but tended toward clean, simple lines in a subdued palette with minimum details.

Youth trends and casual clothes

Throughout all this, the American ready-to-wear market kept quietly expanding, with the emphasis on leisurewear and clothes that combined functionality with good design. The ever-growing teen market was demanding clothes that related to young lives, not their mothers', and the United States was the first country to recognize the business potential of a new consumer group who were very different from adults. Designers began to pay attention. In the 1940s the teenager as a separate entity simply did not exist; young people copied adult taste and wore scaled-down versions of their parents' clothes. But in the 1950s, American companies started to see the financial advantages of creating a separate youth market, and adolescents were targeted with their own products made especially for them. This was the beginning of the young woman being seen as a potent commercial force, whereas previously fashion had always been aimed at a mature woman (between 30 and 40 years of age) of comfortable means.

The most notable young fashions of the time were simple and easily adopted by a broad cross section of people. Marlon Brando, James Dean, and Elvis Presley were influencing teenagers, who increasingly wanted their own style of fashion and music. Rock 'n' roll had arrived, and with it a teenage look of straight black jeans and leather jacket for boys (as exemplified by Marlon Brando in *The Wild One*, 1953) and for girls a "poodle" skirt (a long full skirt with a topstitched poodle on it), bobby socks, saddle shoes, and a tight sweater. The sporty American look of girls in tight slacks, flat ballet-style pumps, and a short-sleeved sweater had a parallel existence at the end of the decade as the Parisian beatniks adopted it as their chic black uniform, worn by the existentialist crowd in smoky jazz clubs and cafés.

OPPOSITE Valentina Sanina operated as Valentina. Here is her 1950 oyster-white silk grosgrain skirt and jacket, with black hat, belt, gloves, and jersey blouse.

ABOVE Suit by Hattie Carnegie in aquamarine-blue wool with a velvet collar and beret, 1952. Carnegie specialized in creating an entire look.

BELOW Strapless evening dress with embroidered red velvet bodice, satin belt, and chiffon skirt, by James Galanos, 1959.

LEFT New York socialite and fashion icon Babe Paley, wearing a blue-and-black dress from Traina-Norell, early 1950s.

BELOW Red knit dress with boat-cut neckline and push-up sleeves by Joseph Guttman, 1950.

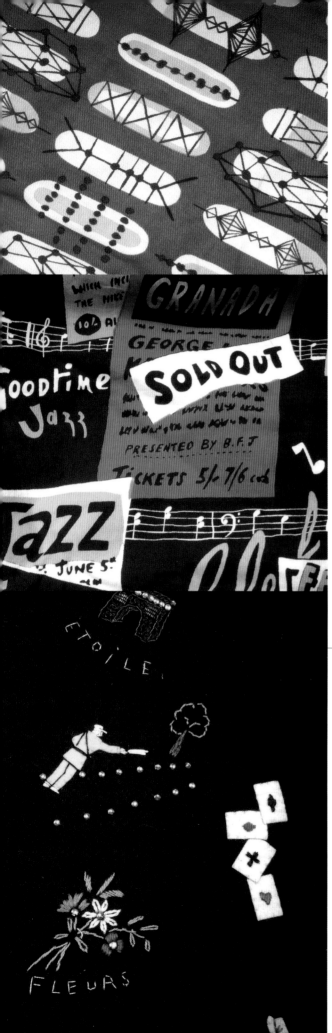

LEFT, TOP TO BOTTOM Atomic print, rock 'n' roll jazz print, and rare American-designed shirt featuring French motifs.

Prints and Fabrics

The 1950s were a decade awash with imaginative prints and surfaces adorned with embroidery and beading – popular for both daywear and glamorous eveningwear. After the drab 1940s, decorative fabrics with highly stylized graphic prints and detailed beading and appliqué stood out as something new and modern. America was the instigator of the explosion in leisurewear and in the popular way that print was used for dresses, circle skirts, and shirtdresses.

New developments in fibers and production resulted in fashion knits, which were adopted by the teen market to wear casually over ski-pants-style slacks and dirndl skirts. Chunky knits with open-neck collars in soft pastel shades of baby blue and canary yellow were staples of weekend leisurewear, and could even be washed by machine. Fine-gauge knits were commonly embellished with complex glass beading, either in a decorative flower pattern along both sides of a cardigan opening or in paisley-style patterns that adorned the cuffs and neckline. Sequins were used in the same way on cardigans and short-sleeved turtleneck sweaters.

Decorative surface detailing was common for day in the form of rickrack braiding and hand embroidery, but for evening, sequins and beads were an essential ingredient of grown-up glamour. Norman Norell created a range of shimmery, sequined dresses that were sheathlike in style with a low neck and cut just above the knee. Strapless prom-style dresses were commonly decorated with sequins or beads around the whole of the bodice area.

Another 1950s staple that people immediately associate with the decade was very loud prints. Used for skirts, slacks, and men's shirts, they ranged from florals to small repeat patterns. The popular shirtwaist dress and gathered skirts, which were fitted tightly around the waist and gently flared out to below the knee, all came in small allover prints, many intricate in design. Circles joined up with triangles and elongated trapezoids all interconnected in different colors on a plain background. Bright floral prints of tulips, roses, and marigolds were common prints for housecoats and circular skirts, especially in hues of bold turquoise, red, and pink.

Leisurewear took off in a big way, and in America the wholesome "girl next door," as typified by Doris Day, often wore a full skirt, which had very stylized graphic prints of cowboys and western paraphernalia, futuristic atomic prints, or small poodle-dog prints. Some of these skirts had handpainted patterns, or dog cutouts made of felt with a collar and pretend chain embroidered onto the fabric. Gaudy prints and colors were also part of the male wardrobe, in the form of short-sleeved Hawaiian shirts, which became standard leisurewear in America, along with boxer-style swimming trunks.

OPPOSITE Paper taffeta dress with a scooped neckline and sash waist in Patou's famed leaf print. Worn with a pale-blue coat of gathered taffeta with narrow neckband and huge sleeves, 1954.

ABOVE AND RIGHT Pink strapless ballerina-length 1950s prom dress. Ideal for dancing and worn with an underskirt, the dress typically featured tiers of net and lace. On the day, the dress would have been worn with a flower corsage at the waist.

Fabrics and synthetics

Mass manufacturing really took off in the 1950s, resulting in the greatest changes for women's clothing in history. The Second World War had seen advances in manufacturing processes and standards of production, all of which were put to good use in the fashion industry when the war was over. For the first part of the century, designers had been restricted to using basic wool, cotton, and silk for their creations, but after the war the developments in man-made fabrics were rapid, and the textile industry provided them with endless new fabric variations to work with.

There are two distinct and defining fabrics that belong to the era. The first is fine English worsted suiting and Irish tweed cloth, as favored by English designers such as Norman Hartnell and Hardy Amies, which were grandly associated with the aristocracy and royalty. These weaves were hugely popular with Parisian designers too because of their finesse and quality, and they were used for the formal suits and coats of the early 1950s. Plaid, houndstooth, and the smaller dogstooth check were perfect for the slim, straight ladylike skirts, and Christian Dior was particularly fond of black-and-white Prince of Wales plaid for his tailored pieces (see also the Worth suit, page 90).

The ongoing production of synthetics was also influential in the development of 1950s fashions. Nylon, which had been used to make parachutes during the war, was continually refined until it became gossamer-thin. It became integral to the look, used to make layers of stiffened petticoats, which supported the circular skirt. Nylon was also fundamental in the development of foundation garments that were becoming increasingly important to the fashion industry. The self-supporting strapless dresses of the time were all kept in place by an elaborate substructure of nylon corseting; and the invention of 12-denier stockings, which were almost invisible, reinforced the stereotypical ladylike image of the period. Today man-made fibers are considered fine for sportswear, but distinctly tawdry for designer clothes; new synthetics such as rayon were seen as miracle fabrics because of their silklike properties to touch, and also because they could hold a shape.

Thick pullovers in baby blue and primrose-yellow acrylic became wardrobe staples worn with a scarf tied at the neck, especially over black stretch pants. Sheer fabrics were very popular for eveningwear, frequently used for decorum on shoulders or arms and as top layers over a solid fabric for dresses and skirts. This stream of new fabrics – acrylic, polyester, acetate, and spandex – changed women's lives, as they were able to indulge in clean clothes every day. Manufacturers enthusiastically produced and promoted polyester blouses in white and pastel colors, promising that they could be easily washed and left to drip-dry in minutes.

RIGHT Strapless 1950s red nylon ballgown from Harrods' own label, England, with pleated bodice and bow detail. Nylon, a new synthetic, was considered a high-end product and perfectly acceptable in designer fashions.

FEATURES OF 1950S PROM DRESSES:

❖ Fitted strapless bodice
❖ Full skirt to below the knee
❖ Tiers of lace and tulle
❖ Synthetic fabrics, such as acrylic and polyester
❖ Colored net petticoats
❖ Fabric or paper corsage worn on the bodice or at the waist
❖ Solid, bright colors
❖ Worn with matching long gloves and loud costume jewelry in the form of brooches or strings of pearls

▼ Gloves
Women wore short kid-leather gloves for formal daywear, and in the evening long satin gloves were worn to complement their strapless cocktail dresses and evening gowns. The fashionable look was to wear them pushed down with big glitzy bracelets over the top.

Slacks
Old-fashioned, ski-pants-style trousers were made of synthetic stretch fabric in solid-colored fabrics or multicolored plaid. Tailored to fit the body, they had a flat front waistband and side zipper opening; they epitomized the casual look in America's growing leisurewear market.

▶ Ballet shoes
Simple flat black pumps based on a classic ballet shoe became popular in 1950s America and Europe. They were mass-produced and worn with ankle socks and full skirts, or with bare feet and cut-off capri pants.

▼ Net petticoats
Layers of petticoats were worn under full skirts to give lift and movement; they were stiffened with starch or a sugar solution to keep their form. Tiered petticoats made from nylon tulle gave a softer look, which was less ballroom-dancing in style. They gave form and volume to many styles of 1950s ballgowns.

Key looks of the decade

1950s

Hats
Pull-down bucket hats, small lampshade-style hats, coolie hats, and wide-brimmed flat picture hats made from colored straw were all popular shapes. Black and white were used to graphic effect and for grand occasions, and women often wore a formal black net veil.

Pencil skirts
A narrow, slim straight skirt called the "hobble," and first pioneered by Poiret, restricted women's walking. It fell from a narrow waistband with little excess fabric, no gathers or pleats, and usually a small back split that allowed for movement.

Empire lines
The little black dress that Givenchy designed for Audrey Hepburn in *Breakfast at Tiffany's* (1961) is a much-copied classic of the era. The straight empire-line shift dress, cut to the knee, with narrow shoulders and a high boat neckline, was given iconic status when she wore it with big black sunglasses and pearls.

Fur stoles
The most popular style of eveningwear was strapless, and the addition of a large fur stole wrapped around bare shoulders, sometimes fastened with a large brooch, became the most fashionable way to keep covered in the evening.

Oversized detailing

The decade's tailoring embraced oversized details, in the form of huge shawl collars, giant buttons, and big turn-back cuffs on wide square-cut sleeves with very deep armholes, known as dolman sleeves.

Trapeze coats

The loose swing coat, which was sometimes called a tent and resembled a triangle in shape, was made to accommodate the wide skirts of the time, and the postwar pregnancy boom. Many were given a diverging set of buttons, designed to emphasize the triangle shape of the cut.

◄Sack dress

The waistless Givenchy sack dress, as modeled here by Audrey Hepburn in 1958, finally freed the figure from the restrictive hourglass.

Sheath dress

The fitted sheath clung to a woman's body shape. In satin or silk, it was usually strapless and required considerable corseting.

Wide belts

A small waist was emphasized for almost every fashionable look throughout the decade. Either with a full dirndl skirt or a straight pencil skirt, or with sporty slacks or capri pants, a big, wide belt was a must-have fashion accessory.

Pedal pushers and capris

Half-length trousers, either cuffed or flounced at the hem, or cut narrow, were prominent, from ready-to-wear to high fashion. Capris were slimline pants, and most had a small V at the hem to enable greater mobility. Here, Natalie Wood models a strapless top and pedal pushers in the 1950s.

▲Full skirts

Wide, circular skirts were worn for daywear in simple fabrics like gingham and printed cottons. They sometimes had big, bold designs, like a poodle or American cowboy motifs, printed on them. For eveningwear full skirts were made from layers of frothy chiffon or rayon in the most vibrant of colors – canary yellow, baby blue, and lime green.

Sweater dressing

The short-sleeved turtleneck, worn tight and fitted, and the big bulky pastel-colored pullover were favorites for teenagers and movie stars alike. The twinset, with its sleeveless crew-necked sweater and matching cardigan with neat pearl buttons and decorative beading, became a 1950s staple,

1960s

The Swinging '60s, as they became known, were an extraordinary decade of change after the conservative ethos of the 1950s. The fashion zeitgeist was changing direction; whereas in previous generations it was always Paris that had led the way, now London took a leading role. When in 1960 a 24-year-old Yves Saint Laurent showed what was to be his final collection for Christian Dior and sent out a cool Beat-inspired collection of black leather suits and knitted caps to an astonished and slightly bewildered audience, he effectively sounded the death knell of French haute couture. With the rumblings of a revolution well under way and a party atmosphere prevailing in London, this was a defining moment when fashion turned a corner. Labels such as "formal" and "casual" dressing, which had existed in the previous decade, ceased to have any meaning at all. As new styles arrived in small London boutiques on a weekly basis, savvy shoppers quickly learned that fresh stock was delivered in the evenings, and they hung around to make sure they were first to grab the latest looks. It was in the 1960s that fashion became absolutely central to a young person's identity. For the first time ever, there was a generation of young people with money to spend, looking for ways to express their newfound sense of freedom through fashion, music, and lifestyle. The generational power balance had shifted: Young people were making things happen for themselves and enjoying doing so, while simultaneously thumbing their noses at the Old Guard.

The British Explosion

Britain – and London in particular – was where everyone wanted to be, and the Youthquake explosion that affected every area of popular culture gathered pace as the decade wore on. It was a time when talented young people, regardless of class or background, were determined to make revolutionary changes and demand recognition for what they did. Image was everything; fresh-faced photographers such as David Bailey, Terence Donovan, and Brian Duffy changed the style of photography from formal studio-based portraiture to energetic street-style "reality." The models they worked with – Twiggy, Jean Shrimpton (the Shrimp), and Verushka – became icons of their time for their playful poses and quirky looks.

The Beatles and the Rolling Stones changed the look and sound of music, and on the streets there were new and exciting boutiques springing up on London's Carnaby Street and King's Road. Typically small, dark, and deafeningly loud with the pop music of the day, they flourished overnight and in many cases simply disappeared just as quickly. Owned and run by ambitious individuals, they were united by the weirdest of names: Granny Takes A Trip, Mr Freedom, Hung On You, and I Was Lord Kitchener's Valet. Fashion was no longer dictated by middle-aged Parisian designers, and the demand by London's young "dolly birds" to wear whatever they wanted, whenever and wherever they felt like it, was being met by a host of up-and-coming British design stars who were spilling out from art schools. The Royal College of Art fashion department was run by Professor Jayney Ironside, who became a legendary figure for her ability to spot and nurture a generation of young talents, many of whom went on to become internationally famous. Zandra Rhodes, Bill Gibb, Ossie Clark, Marion Foale, and Sally Tuffin were all students under her tutelage. These and many others – including Gina Fratini, Anthony Price, Yuki, and Thea Porter – were part of a mushrooming band of designers who were responsible for turning London into a leading fashion capital. Not all the hip young things who were helping to build Britain's fashionable reputation had a fashion degree; some had simply arrived at the same place by a different route.

Mary Quant, undoubtedly an early trailblazer of the Youthquake movement, had studied illustration at Goldsmiths College before setting up a tiny shop in 1955 with her then boyfriend and business partner, Alexander Plunkett-Green. Barbara Hulanicki, the owner and designer behind the hugely influential Biba boutiques, started out as a fashion illustrator before deciding to try designing something she liked instead of illustrating other people's clothes. Jean Muir, who went on to become one of the leading British names for understated classics, started out as a sketcher for Jaeger.

PAGE 112 Model, muse, and icon Twiggy in a gold-and-orange striped minidress in the 1960s.

OPPOSITE A 1960s advertisement for Mary Quant dresses in the new fiber acrylic (British trade name Courtelle). The classic minidress featured a zipper down the front with a circular pull-ring.

RIGHT AND BELOW Mary Quant's Prince-of-Wales plaid dress for Ginger Group. This was made for her less expensive, mass-produced line of coordinates in 1963. Her miniskirt and Chelsea look became the most defining fashion features of the decade.

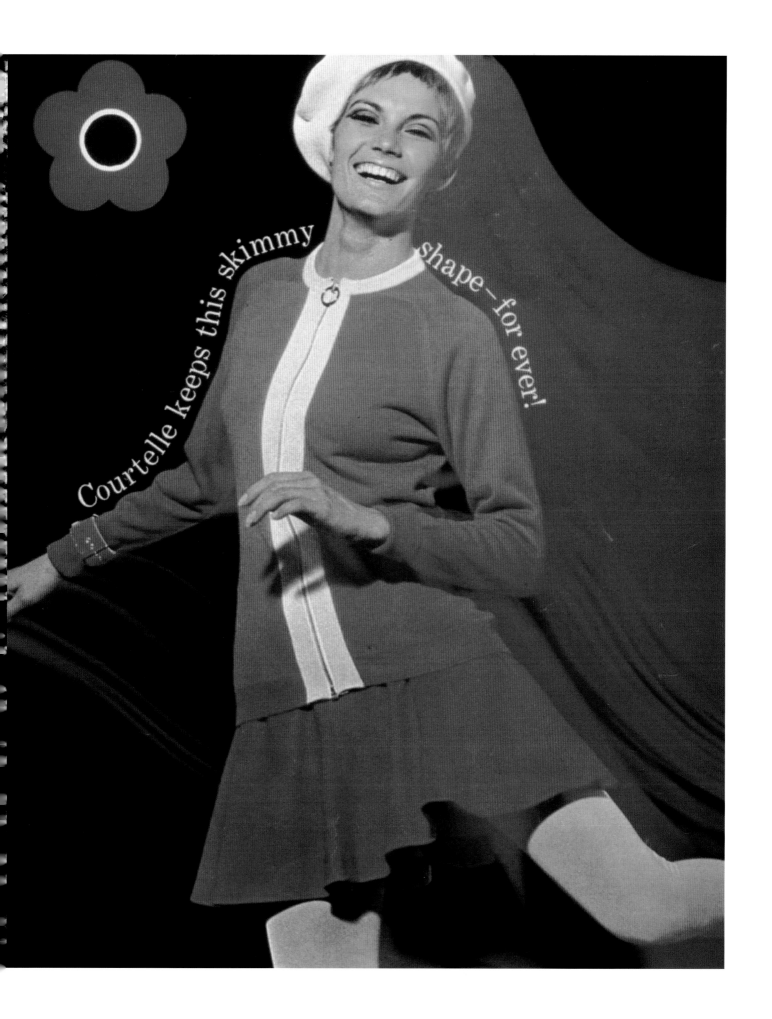

Courtelle keeps this skimmy shape – for ever!

SIGNATURE BIBA ELEMENTS:

❖ Droopy low-cut necklines with ties
❖ Button detailing, as long rows of covered buttons on cuffs or at the neck
❖ Leg-of-mutton sleeves
❖ Allover small prints
❖ Funnel collars with buttons
❖ Bias cutting on long dresses
❖ Colored fake-fur shrugs and tippets
❖ Maxi-length double-breasted trench coats

LEFT Model wearing a Biba op art jumpsuit outside the Abingdon Road shop in London, 1967.

Biba

The Biba label was a huge success in Britain from the time Barbara Hulanicki opened her first little shop in 1964 on Abingdon Road, London, until the demise of the Biba lifestyle store on Kensington High Street in 1975. Hulanicki broke all the rules for dressing. She created whole outfits, including a matching makeup range, which meant that people could dress entirely in Biba. Hats, scarves, underwear, pantyhose, and shoes could all be bought in the same soft muted colors to create an entire look from head to toe — something no other designer had considered at the time.

From her initial mail-order catalog, called Biba's Postal Boutique, which she and her business manager-husband Stephen Fitz Simon started in 1963, the Biba style offered a unique look for young women. The clothes were cheap, which made them even more desirable for the young working-class customer who wanted to dress fashionably. For the same price as a Mary Quant dress, a girl could walk out of Biba with a new coat, dress, shoes, and hat. The Biba look was also overtly soft and feminine (not the short, sharp, angular tailoring of other 1960s designers), with droopy collars, gathered-in sleeves, flared skirts, and long-line vests. Daywear fabrics often had an allover small print, either miniature floral sprays reminiscent of 1940s tea dresses or zigzag geometric designs. Fabrics for

daywear tended to be soft wool jersey or crepe — fabrics that allowed movement and gathering. Trademark design elements were big leg-of-mutton sleeves, falling tightly into long cuffs with rows of covered buttons, long rounded collars, and vests with flared panels, cut to the same length as the miniskirt. For evening, Hulanicki's obsession with the glamorous 1920s and 1930s resulted in her 1960s mixture of art nouveau and art deco. She favored dark smudgy colors, from the black and gold of the Biba logo to chocolate brown, all shades of grape, and smudgy deep gray-blue. Fabrics were shiny satins and panne velvet, topped off with a matching feather boa. By the early 1970s, leopard skin was big, worn with wide fake-fur collars and shrugs.

When Biba closed its doors in 1975, few people would have imagined that the designs would become collectors' items. At the time, they were seen as the fashion equivalent of the rock 'n' roll epitaph "Live Fast, Die Young," clothes that were fantastically appropriate for their immediacy but with little ongoing mileage. They were, of course, incredibly cheap and notoriously badly made, which suited the customer of the time. Twenty years ago, Biba pieces could be found at rummage sales and secondhand market stalls. Now they are seen as covetable pieces of history.

ABOVE AND OPPOSITE LEFT Art-deco print rayon late-1960s Biba dress, with a pussycat-bow tie neckline. Past eras, such as the art deco and Edwardian periods, were evident in Barbara Hulanicki's designs, which eventually included housewares and interiors as well as clothes.

ABOVE AND LEFT Psychedelic heart-print motif 1967-8 Biba suit from the Abingdon Road shop, featuring a neat line of buttons. Loud and clashing colored prints were snapped up by the decade's hip young things.

Space-Age Design

Where London led, Paris followed, and soon the *prêt-à-porter* collections of young Parisian designers were generating new headlines around the fashion world. Inspired by the Yuri Gagarin spaceflight in 1961, such designers as André Courrèges and Pierre Cardin produced futuristic collections using a limited color palette of shimmering white and silver. These space-age clothes, based on a fantasy vision of life in the year 2000, were modernistic, minimal, and designed around straight shapes and clean-cut lines. Superfluous decoration was discarded in favor of A-line tunics, short straight skirts, and flat kid-leather boots.

When French designer André Courrèges showed his Moon Girl collection in 1964, it was a show that was defined by straight lines and boxy shapes without a ruffle in sight. Simplicity was the key, and he offered lean pantsuits with straight-legged pants that had a slit up the front seam to fall open over his flat boots; square-cut coats with very little detailing, mostly single-breasted with simple pocket tabs at the hips; and the shortest miniskirts in Paris. Accessories of white,

ABOVE AND BELOW Lime-and-white 1960s Courrèges jacket with inside collar label. The jacket exhibits the Bauhaus-influenced designer's streamlined, modernist structuring. By inserting rounded forms into his designs, he created a curvilinear shape.

OPPOSITE Red-and-white ready-to-wear fashions designed by André Courrèges, 1968.

oversized goggle sunglasses and smooth helmet-style hats completed the Moon Girl look. Freedom of movement was paramount, and his young models, all in white kid boots, strode down the catwalks with a purposeful bounce.

The hard, straight lines of these clothes, together with the angular girls who were wearing them, led inevitably to unisex clothing. Sonny and Cher appeared together in his-and-hers striped hipster pants that were cut low across the hips and worn with a big belt, fringed leather vests, and simple T-shirts. It was a must-have look for young couples who wanted to appear identical and share everything.

The hugely talented Yves Saint Laurent was one of the few designers able to make the leap from the sumptuous postwar Paris of the 1950s to the youthful vigor and freedom required by fashion in the 1960s. Having started in haute couture for the house of Dior, he quickly embraced the breakdown of the old society and invented Rive Gauche, his ready-to-wear label, in 1962. As a designer who found inspiration from a world in transition, he exerted a considerable influence throughout the decade. From an early collection based on Mondrian's geometric blocks of color and graphic black lines used on a white jersey tunic dress, to his motif moon, heart, and face pop art dresses, and later his vivid gypsy collection, Saint Laurent's collections captured the mood of the street in a stylized way. Many of his designs, such as safari jackets and transparent dresses, became staples that transcended the decade. Most importantly his 1966 classic tuxedo suit for women, "Le Smoking," paved the way to androgynous fashion and 1980s power suits.

SPACE-AGE STYLES:

- Mini-jumpers
- Graphic black-and-white designs and prints
- White and silver plastic
- Plastic detailing
- Metal-chain dresses, tops, and tunics
- Metal jewelry incorporated into dresses, especially at the neckline
- Cutouts in dresses and trousers
- Oversized patch pockets
- Asymmetric cutting
- See-through mesh
- Vinyl coats, trousers, and dresses

OPPOSITE White Louis Féraud minidress with cutouts, late 1960s. After his 1960 catwalk collection, Féraud was contracted to Oleg Cassini, which made him available to North America and Britain.

RIGHT Louis Féraud white minidress with silver bead cutouts, late 1960s. White-and-silver combinations were used to create a futuristic look and denote youth and newness.

LEFT Silver late-1960s dress by Youthquake, an American label sold through the Paraphernalia shops. Youthquake, a term coined by *Vogue*'s editor-in-chief Diana Vreeland in 1963, was a 1960s movement that embraced fashion, music, and popular culture, and was centered on London.

Paco Rabanne took the space-age idea even further by creating clothes from materials not normally associated with fashion. Plastic disks, pieces of scrap metal, and chain mail were all crafted into angular shapes, which were thought of as half sculpture, half fashion.

His unusual approach to fashion came about ostensibly because he had trained to be an architect, not a fashion designer, although during his student years he had sold fashion-accessory sketches to Courrèges, Cardin, and Balenciaga, who had all encouraged his creativity. In 1966 Rabanne produced a resolutely modern collection of 12 experimental and slightly unwearable dresses, which were shown on barefoot models who danced down the catwalk to loud music. Using a rigid plastic called Rhodoid, metal, pliers, and a blowtorch, he eliminated sewing and created clothing by positioning a model on his work table and shaping metal parts onto her body. His experimental creations were very much in keeping with what young modern women wanted to be seen in, and Rabanne continued to innovate with paper dresses in 1967, and later seamless dresses, made by spraying vinyl chloride onto preshaped molds. He will be remembered for his 1969 gold-metal sculptured dress and for his costumes for Jane Fonda in the sci-fi movie *Barbarella*.

Simple Shapes and Cuts

The many exciting designers who burst into production at the start of the 1960s were determined that young people should have their own voice when it came to fashion, and that they should be allowed to express themselves visually in a way that reflected the changes in society. For the first time in history – with the exception of Coco Chanel's unrestricted jersey collections in the 1930s – women's clothing was to become comfortable and easy to wear. For most of the decade designers had a very simple mantra, and that was to worship the God of Simplicity. The "mods" of the early 1960s were ardent devotees of this creed, deeply concerned with their immaculate appearance. They were almost fanatical about their "uniform" of pointy shoes and narrow straight-legged trousers, worn with a buttondown shirt and a very simple jacket, which had three buttons at the front and two vents at the back.

Shift dresses and tunics

Mary Quant's early output was based on very straight simple shift dresses, which bypassed the waist (such a focus of attention in the previous decade) and simply hung to above the knee. These were clothes that were easy to pull on and run to catch a bus in. Hemlines quickly rose to mid-thigh, but shapes remained very simple, with neat A-line coats, jersey sweater dresses that clung to the body, and endless sleeveless tunics with high-cut armholes and narrow shoulders.

Rudi Gernreich and Pierre Cardin were just two of many designers who produced countless variations on a straight tunic shape – big cutaway armholes, outsized circular pockets, and contrasting edging were all devices that added visual impact to what was essentially a simple sleeveless dress. It helped, of course, that girls all aspired to look like Twiggy – flat-chested, legs like a gazelle, and hardly any bottom. The "no body" body was perfect for hanging unstructured clothes on, as they needed to fit only where they touched; the fragile waif was the ideal shape to wear skinny ribbed sweaters – hugely popular at the time.

The miniskirt

From the daring tunic dress that fell to the knee, it was a short way to the straight square-cut. Hemlines continued to rise from just above the knee in 1963 to six inches above the knee by the end of 1965. By the end of the decade, the mini was barely more than a large hipster belt, and it became known as the micromini. The only way to go from here was down. By 1969 it was common to see girls with long ankle-length maxi coats worn over tiny hotpants and microminis with patterned pantyhose and clunky square-heeled patent shoes.

OPPOSITE Yves Saint Laurent handknitted smock dresses with diamond-patterned bodice and sleeves, hem and yoke all in one color, 1966. The dress on the far left has a turtleneck and the other a round neck. Saint Laurent's daring color combinations and interest in geometrics and modern art can be appreciated in this distinctive pattern.

ABOVE Orange Pierre Cardin suit, late 1960s, with circular shaped detailing. Cardin's simple modernist lines were echoed in the work of André Courrèges, and both men had a deep fascination with futuristic ideas – sharp geometric cuts in necklines, hems, and pocket details that seemed to owe more to architecture than to dressmaking.

Knitwear and key advances

New developments in the textile industry were exploited for body-conscious clothing, especially nylon and woolly patterned pantyhose, both of which had just been invented and looked fantastic with the miniskirt, as long as they were worn by girls who were tall and slim.

In Europe, a diminutive, style-conscious Frenchwoman named Sonia Rykiel began designing comfortable but desirable clothes for herself when she became pregnant. Her design status grew very quickly, and her specialty became knitwear, making use of modern technology to produce very fine-gauge sweaters in myriad distinctive colors and stripes. By 1964, Rykiel had been nicknamed the Queen of Knitwear in the U.S., where she acquired an army of fans for her skinny-knit sweater dresses and cardigans.

In Italy, the Missoni family, who had started their knitwear business in 1953, was also producing clothes that were grabbing worldwide attention for their fluidity and imaginative use of color. Throughout the 1960s and 1970s, Ottavio ("Tai") and Rosita Missoni helped seal Milan's growing reputation as a fashionable epicenter with their artistic collection of knits. Unlike old-fashioned hand knits, which were heavy and bulky, Missoni pieces were exceptionally lightweight, with patterns that included stripes, zigzags, and even patchwork. Missoni used modern machinery to produce unimaginable artistry in its pieces, which were often compared to works of art. Such was the success of some of the original Missoni pieces that the house has reissued modern copies of the early lines.

Trousers and suits

Interestingly, pants became fashionable for town wear and even, in suitable fabrics, for dressy occasions. Even so, they were at first somewhat controversial in class-conscious Britain, where they were perceived by some as working-class clothing: Many London restaurants refused entry to women wearing them. Only after a television presenter, Cathy McGowan, wore them on a game show in 1963 did they suddenly become acceptable.

It was the decade of the leg – either revealed by the micromini or defined by trousers. In Britain, Tuffin and Foale were among the first designers to create a mix-and-match trouser and miniskirt option, which provided the customer with the choice of what to wear with the jacket, a revolutionary idea at the time.

Straight-legged skinny pants, loose 1930s pajama-style trousers, and wide flares were all acceptable shapes during the decade. As the "waistless" dress evolved into the tunic, so the design of trousers became much lower cut, sitting on the hips instead of the waist – hence the name "hipsters," which were the popular unisex choice for skinny boys and girls from 1965. As the decade progressed, flares became increasingly voluminous, to the point where they were cut like full-length culottes.

OPPOSITE Narrow-cut corduroy Tuffin and Foale pantsuit from 1964. Sally Tuffin and Marion Foale produced clothes that had a street-style appeal and celebrated youth culture.

BELOW Fabric-covered snaps on the Dior suit, a distinctive sign of a couture garment.

LEFT Christian Dior lime-and-pink plaid suit, 1960s. Although the great master was no longer alive, his house continued to keep step with the times, as seen in the fluffy, tactile tweed and modern cut. Note the short half-pockets at the jacket's hem.

A Feminine Design Ethic

Running parallel to the modern line of André Courrèges and Pierre Cardin were numerous designers who embraced a much more feminine design ethic and who were producing decidedly girlish clothes with ruffles and gathers and a much softer line. Emilio Pucci, the darling of the international jet set, with his lurid-print, loose-cut caftan shapes, bell-sleeved tops, and pajama pants, became famous for clothes that relied on a much looser shape and cut. By mid-decade there was also a definite swing to a modern interpretation of old-fashioned Hollywood glamour, and much of Biba's success was built upon Barbara Hulanicki's individual take on 1920s and '30s style. When she started Biba, she was fond of low-cut necklines, wide loose pants, short flared skirts, and women's shirts with exaggerated high collars and full sleeves. As the Biba phenomenon grew, she became known for long bias-cut dresses with feather boas and maxi-length trench coats with big floppy hats.

Influences from the past

Other designers looked to different eras for inspiration. Gina Fratini and Bellville Sassoon were two who became renowned for high romanticism. Their designs contained an element of graceful, innocent femininity.

Laura Ashley was a British designer who achieved long-lasting success with her brand of Old World nostalgia. Integrating ideas from Edwardian and Victorian clothing, she produced a range of rustic country-girl clothes reminiscent of a Thomas Hardy heroine. Pin-tucked bodices, tiered skirts, full puff-sleeved blouses, and long ruffled smocks were all trademark pieces that came in Ashley's own prints. Her reinterpretation of original eighteenth- and nineteenth-century patterns, floral sprigs and paisleys that were printed on fine lawn in subtle color combinations, provided her with a look that was instantly recognized and highly coveted on both sides of the Atlantic.

SIGNATURE LAURA ASHLEY ELEMENTS:
* High Edwardian-style necklines
* Full sleeves gathered from the shoulder into a long cuff
* Rows of covered "ball" buttons on cuffs of sleeves
* Liberty-print lawn
* Pin-tucked bodices
* Lace trim
* Tiered skirts
* Floral-sprig prints
* Long smocks
* Frilled aprons

OPPOSITE Laura Ashley prints evoked the natural beauty of the Welsh countryside with florals, paisleys, and small romantic prints, which provided a rustic charm and natural simplicity. Her designs reworked influences from past eras, and her florals were usually printed in just two colors, but in many different combinations.

RIGHT An early-1960s Laura Ashley minidress with a button opening at the front. The rigid tunic shape would be replaced by her famous Victorian-style maxi dresses in the late 1960s and '70s.

The hippie look and the antifashion movement

The last years of the decade exploded in a riot of color and confusion as the fashion pendulum swung from the simplified lines of 1960s modern London to the nostalgic secondhand clothes of the hippies, which lasted into the early 1970s.

Pop music gave way to rock, and the international hit "San Francisco (Be Sure to Wear Some Flowers in Your Hair)" was the anthem for a generation of festival-goers who painted daisies on their faces, extolled the virtues of free love, and invented a street style of utilitarian and ethnic clothes. There was a confusion of gender; young couples shared everything, including their embroidered jeans, and copied each other's look, from long hair to granny glasses.

Escapism in the form of secondhand clothes included styles from everywhere: caftans from India, American workers' jeans, Chairman Mao jackets, Afghan jackets and vests, and ex-army regimental uniforms (as worn by the Beatles for the *Sergeant Pepper* album). The hippie look was not a designer's creation; it was about individuality, as everything was picked up from secondhand market stalls and no two people could wear identical outfits. However, this antifashion movement, inspired by psychedelic drugs and nostalgia, provided a springboard for such British designers as Zandra Rhodes, Thea Porter, and Ossie Clark, and in the United States, for Giorgio di Sant'Angelo and Bill Blass.

Drawing on myriad influences from the past, such as beaded dresses from the 1920s and bias-cut slips with handkerchief hemlines from the 1930s, these designers specialized in beautifully crafted clothes. Their signature pieces were fantasy dresses, embellished with embroidery, quilting, and beading. Print was important, as were softer flowing lines, gathered sleeves, and fuller shapes that were the antithesis of the short, square-cut lines that had been popular for most of the previous decade.

Other designers who chose to operate outside the system and create their own vision of alternative world clothing were Jean Bouquin, who opened a Bedouin palace–influenced shop in the South of France crammed with luxurious caftans, loose baggy pants, and exotic African beads.

In London in 1966, Thea Porter opened a small, dark shop on Soho's Greek Street, initially full of opulent interior pieces as well as a few ethnic robes, which were brought in from Damascus, her hometown, in the Middle East. The shop became a mecca for young student types who wanted to embrace everything Eastern. As the items she imported sold out quickly, Porter decided to design her own dresses to meet demands. Her versions of loose flowing gowns and caftans that grazed the floor were made in a variety of brocades, velvets, and lightweight chiffons often recycled from traditional Eastern textiles and were popular with royalty and the international jet set. Although inspired by the Middle

RIGHT AND OPPOSITE INSET Indian silk, empire-line Thea Porter dress with crimson sleeves trimmed in black velvet, late 1960s. Derived from Middle Eastern and Indian costume, Porter's dresses had easy, flattering shapes and full skirts, which worked several patterns together in one piece.

OPPOSITE Rippled blue silk caftan printed with large peonies over pink silk taffeta pants by Bill Blass, 1965. Blass was known for his ability to mix pattern and texture.

East, Thea Porter's designs were her own romantic interpretation of the exotic, and as fashion moved on rapidly, so did she, later producing collections that drew on the last days of the Russian empire, gypsy flounces, and even an exotic knitwear range that was specifically made for the cold English climate.

Ossie Clark, who graduated from the Royal College of Art in London, in 1965, was a master cutter who had an artistic vision and possessed the technical skill to turn it into a reality. He found the miniskirt restrictive and instead concentrated on clothes that were flattering to the female body. His collaboration with his wife, the textile designer Celia Birtwell, produced inspirational fashion, and their work together won them instant success. He favored crepe, jersey, and chiffon because of their fluidity and produced clothes that combined intensely complex cutting techniques with a variety of prints, all used on the same garment. At the time, this was a revolutionary approach to womenswear, and his clothes were coveted by all the glitterati; special commissions were made for Bianca Jagger, Britt Ekland, and Verushka. Loose pajama-style pants in fabulous printed silk, bias-cut chiffon dresses with very full sleeves gathering into a tight cuff, quilted paneling, and high-cut, oval-shaped waistbands are all Ossie Clark trademarks.

ABOVE Late 1960s Ossie Clark silk dress in a blue-and-red Celia Birtwell print on a cream field. Clark's imaginative cutting marked a shift from hard-edged modernism to feminine romanticism in the 1960s.

RIGHT In the late 1960s Ossie Clark collaborated with the photographer Jim Lee in developing groundbreaking new ways to present his clothes. The Airplane dress, featured above left, is seen here in a 1969 Jim Lee photograph.

Textiles and Prints

The rapid technological developments in the textile industry in the 1960s led to an unprecedented choice of materials that had never been used before in the fashion industry. Manufacturers had started to develop new easy-care, easy-to-wear fabrics that incorporated polyester. These brand-new fabrics were comfortable to touch, wrinkle free, and required very little time to look after them; in fact, they were a perfect match for the simple miniskirts and short tunic dresses of the era. As the radical change in womenswear continued, designers like Emanuel Ungaro and Paco Rabanne looked to more unconventional materials such as paper, plastic, and metal to use instead of soft fabrics. Their choice of material limited their design, but plastic chain mail, with its hard and resolutely modern feel, was a perfect choice for the avant-garde creations of the Parisian haute couture designers.

Mary Quant and Yves Saint Laurent were both fans of another new material that had been borrowed from industrial usage and reinvented as a fashion fabric. Vinyl (also called PVC) was a shiny, wet-look plastic that was easy to color and print with flamboyant designs, and also looked exactly right for the times, as it was available in plain black or white. It became hugely popular with teenage girls, and required nothing more than a rub down with a damp cloth to keep it looking good. At first it was used for outerwear: double-breasted belted raincoats, knee-high boots, and shiny newsboy caps; then for every style of clothing, from zip-up bomber jackets, bags, and belts to tunics and miniskirts.

As the formality of dressing continued to break down, designers abandoned the traditional rules of when and where a particular type of fabric should be worn. Fabrics that had previously been restricted to eveningwear or special-occasion dressing were now used extensively for ordinary clothes. Velvet, brocade, satin, and lace began to be used for daywear, and it became perfectly acceptable to wear the same outfit to work and then later on for an evening out.

Graphic lines and op art

The severity of the A-line tunic, and short boxy jackets and coats, provided a perfect canvas for the equally strong dynamic of using just black and white as a colorway. Fashion in the 1960s tended to be very graphic. John Bates, a British designer who provided all of Diana Rigg's costumes for the cult television

OPPOSITE Dresses by Paco Rabanne featuring dots, chevrons, checks, and apple motifs, 1966.

series *The Avengers,* knew how visually powerful this could be. Using only black and white for bold stripes, checks, and diagonal chevrons, he designed a set of clothes for the character Emma Peel that sparked headlines in nearly every daily paper in Britain. Graphic stripes, dots, checks, and zebra print then turned into hypnotic illusions; suddenly, the influence of such op artists as Bridget Riley and Frank Stella filtered through to the fashion industry.

The term *op art* was coined for the dramatic, trick-optic effects of line and contrasting areas of line and color, and fashion designers picked up this art trend and modified it for use in their clothing designs. André Courrèges, Pierre Cardin, Emanuel Ungaro, and Julian Tomchin were all influenced by op art and abstract art movements; Yves Saint Laurent, inspired by the paintings of Mondrian, designed geometric patterns in a celebrated line of Mondrian dresses, following with pop art dresses, in 1966, decorated with comic strips.

BELOW Paper dress with swirly psychedelic design from the 1960s. Although they could be worn only a few times, paper dresses enabled women to try out the latest designs. Now collector's items, they evolved from NASA's experiments with single-use clothing, which made them part of the futuristic theme of the decade.

Psychedelia and Emilio Pucci

Every fashionable trend provokes a polar opposite, and the backlash against stark monochrome minimalism came in the form of psychedelia. By the mid-1960s designers were drawing inspiration from the "flower power" movement and a cacophony of street styles that combined ethnic pieces with Union Jack prints and as much superfluous decoration as possible. Flowered brocades, embroidery, braid, and fringe were all used to create an extraordinarily flamboyant look that was as popular with men as it was with young girls. Clashing colors and big swirly patterns became the fashionable embodiment of a hallucinogenic LSD trip. Carnaby Street in London became a jumble of mismatched prints and styles. In Britain, John Stephen was one of the first to produce completely matching unisex outfits, using wild prints and vibrant colors. Although the young men who wore these clothes had to fight fears of being branded homosexual, ruffled silk shirts, paisley ties, and caftan-style suits made from Eastern prints with mandarin collars were soon being copied for the mass market.

On the continent, Italian designer Emilio Pucci was creating a collection that relied on strong, swirling patterns on simple elegant clothes. A natural stylist, he began by designing his own ski outfit, which was spotted by a *Harper's Bazaar* editor who asked him to design women's skiwear for her to photograph for a story. The look of ski clothes changed forever, and a new fashion empire was established. Using gaudy, vibrant colors and luxury fabrics, Pucci's psychedelic clothes defined the jet set age of the 1960s and were favorites with the cognoscenti on both sides of the Atlantic, with Elizabeth Taylor, Twiggy, and Joan Collins all proud to be part of Puccimania. The thin silk jersey dresses, palazzo pants, and beachwear were wrinkle-resistant and easy to pack, perfect for the international traveler. The designs were heady whirls of color, often bordered by graphic geometrics, and the unmistakable Pucci print became instantly recognizable for generations to come; it was even featured in the logo of the *Apollo 15* space mission

ABOVE, RIGHT, AND BELOW RIGHT Yellow-and-orange silk Pucci psychedelic-print shirt and pants, late 1960s. These palazzo pajamas would usually have been worn with jeweled sandals. Pucci's swirling patterns and unmistakable colors earned him the title Prince of Prints.

OPPOSITE Model Susan Murray wearing a slit print skirt and thin-strapped top by Emilio Pucci, 1966. In the 1960s Pucci produced capri pants, shorts, resort dresses, silk shirts, trousers, and suits, as well as ranges of underwear, sweaters, and swimwear for American manufacturers. He pioneered the color revolution of the decade.

and the interior of a Ford Lincoln Continental. Beloved of Americans, Pucci had a long association with the department store Neiman Marcus, which enabled him to progress from selling his clothing in his boutique on the island of Capri (and making all of the clothing in his own home) to major manufacturing. Pucci's designs and fabrics were kept to an incredibly high quality, and he oversaw all his production houses. He was one of the first designers to sign their name in print on the exterior of his clothes, and the Emilio Pucci signature can be seen on original pieces.

The psychedelic revolution

By 1966 the clashing colors and gaudy rummage-sale attire that had begun life on London's Carnaby Street had started to lose its way stylistically. For a brief period, a new movement appeared, nicknamed the "psychedelic revolution." Starting in the United States, it revolved around music and the hallucinogenic drug LSD. Swirling colors, kaleidoscopic patterns, and a multitude of dizzy-making prints all collided onto unisex shirts, tunics, caftans, and, surprisingly, men's suits. In London the designer Michael Fish, who traded under "Mr. Fish," had opened a tailor's shop that specialized in making fitted suits for men in the most garish stripes and paisleys. He was also responsible for inventing the oversized necktie, often in the same flamboyant fabric to match his shirts and suits.

In the United States, counterculture guru Timothy Leary's words of advice to "turn on, tune in, and drop out" reflected a general desire to reject Western culture and seek inspiration from the East. Young people, with their newfound power in society, wanted to embrace

LEFT, RIGHT, AND BELOW RIGHT
A late-1960s Neiman Marcus copy of a Christian Dior psychedelic-print silk pantsuit. Note the sleeve slits and ties at the wrist.

Chanel Indian lamé pantsuit, 1969. Here, a traditional paisley pattern is reworked in an elaborately trimmed garment, marrying the ethnic influences and psychedelic interests of the time.

ABOVE An orange-and-green psychedelic Lurex tunic and trousers with an orange silk shirt by Apple, the London clothes boutique set up by the Beatles in 1967. The shop lasted for only one year; it closed in July 1968 and gave away the stock.

everything Eastern, from religion to traditional dress, and many European designers were quick to catch on. In 1967, Yves Saint Laurent showed vibrant paisley prints lavished with heavy fringe, Chanel used heavily embellished Indian fabrics for Nehru-style jackets, and Italian designer Count Sarmi produced an opulent evening collection of chiffon harem pants and gold embroidered tunics.

The psychedelic revolution quickly turned into the flower-power movement, inspired by the folk-rock music of Bob Dylan, Joan Baez, and the Byrds. With a peace medallion as their symbol, hundreds of young hippies took off to far-flung regions in a hodgepodge of tie-dyed skirts, collarless "grandad" shirts, paisley headbands, and crushed-velvet patchwork vests. The bohemian hippie style was commercialized by such British designers as Ossie Clark and Zandra Rhodes, while Yves Saint Laurent launched his own layered skirt and peasant blouse in 1969 and Giorgio di Sant'Angelo produced a stunning collection of vibrant gypsy skirts that incorporated fringe, beading, and multicolored sashes.

BELOW AND RIGHT Turquoise silk blouse from the British boutique Granny Takes A Trip, 1967–8. Victorian influences can be seen in its leg-of-mutton sleeves and long row of buttons – historical referencing such as this was commonplace in the decade's designs as past prints, textiles, and detailing were plundered.

▶Space-age looks

With the moon landing came an avalanche of space-age clothes, best exemplified by Courrèges with his all-white Moon Girl collection in 1964. Space-inspired helmets in felted wool or white leather completed the look, as modeled here by Audrey Hepburn, 1965, in Courrèges.

Miniskirts

André Courrèges, in Paris, and Mary Quant, in London, can both lay claim to the invention of the miniskirt. Hemlines started creeping higher at the start of the decade, but by 1965 they had risen to mid-thigh and were to become even shorter. Often worn with a big belt hung loosely over the hips, they were adopted by women around the world, not just the young and leggy.

Hosiery

Innovations in the textile industry saw the invention of all-in-one nylon pantyhose, which gave women much more freedom than stockings and garters had. With the emphasis firmly directed onto the leg, pantyhose quickly became an integral part of the look. They were made in strong colors, with thick stripes, printed patterns, and plaid for winter; white lacy versions were worn under summer dresses.

Key looks of the decade

1960

▼Graphic lines

Miniskirts, shift dresses, and short A-line coats were all given the op art look as fashion reflected the optical illusions of Bridget Riley's paintings. Thick and thin stripes and geometric checks were used to create strong graphic impact in many of the pared-down simple shapes. Here, Natalie Wood models Yves Saint Laurent's Mondrian dress.

▲Synthetics

Polyester, nylon, and other man-made fabrics permitted the wearer movement even with slim-cut styles. This 1966 dress by New York designer Gayle Kirkpatrick, modeled by actress Pamela Tiffin, was made in a special stretch nylon developed by Stretchnit.

▲Boots

It was a decade of boots in vario shapes and styles. Shiny patent boots that came up to and over the knee, in black, white, and silv were the trendiest footwear to g with the mini. The other strong boot shape, which originated in Paris, was a mid-calf white kidski boot with a pointy toe and no heel, sometimes with a flat ribbon and bow around the top

Chain mail

[P]aco Rabanne's resolutely [m]odern designs were made [fr]om a variety of unconventional [m]aterials. Plastic chain mail and [al]uminum appeared in silver, [bl]ack, or white. Difficult to work [w]ith, chain mail projected a [fu]turistic image that was very [m]uch in tune with what women [w]anted. The chain mail and mesh [ca]tsuit below twins chain mail [w]ith the trend for transparency.

Psychedelia

By the middle to late 1960s, the emphasis had shifted from London to America, and more specifically to the flower children of San Francisco, with their anti-Vietnam chants, long hair, and ragbag of utilitarian and ethnic garments. Brocade jeans, frilly shirts, flower-print tunics, Mao jackets, and Indian scarves became a street style emulated by most European designers.

◀ Sheer and transparent

Bodies became the center of attention with transparent panels of clear plastic or meshlike netting, as in the chain-mail catsuit here. Toward the end of the decade, see-through clothes became more daring, with Yves Saint Laurent's sheer black chiffon blouse and Ossie Clark's gossamer-fine chiffon dresses showing more barely covered flesh than ever before.

▶ Plastics

Shiny vinyl was used for every item of clothing from over-the-knee boots to mini-raincoats, bags, and jumpers. It was easy to color and to overprint with bold motifs. Connecting circles of hard plastic were popular for belts and earrings. Shown here, a flowery 1967 dress made of vinyl, plastic, and steel, by Paco Rabanne.

Oversized sunglasses

Huge bug-eyed sunglasses in shiny black or white plastic were one of the hottest accessories to match op art and space-age styles. Perfectly round and goggle-like, they were worn more for photographic styling and celebrity "disguise" than for everyday streetwear.

Maxi and midi lengths

Long coats, skirts, and dresses were designed as the antidote to the mini. The maxi fell to the ankle, and the midi was cut to mid-calf. Women were given much more choice to decide which length they felt comfortable in, and they often chose to wear both at the same time: midi knitted cardigans were worn over short skirts with boots to show a fleeting glimpse of leg.

Cutouts

[Sh]apes were cut out of dresses, [an]d especially to reveal the [mi]dsection. Here, a 1965 design [by] John Bates teams a simple [sh]ift dress with cutout stockings [de]corated with roses and bows.

Shift dresses

The most popular shape was an A-line shift, which fell in a clean triangular line from shoulder to mid-thigh. Big circular pockets, cutaway armholes, and contrasting edging around the neck, hem, and armholes were defining features. Some were designed to wear over a skinny ribbed sweater and ribbed pantyhose during the day, or only with heels in the evening.

1970s

Clothes with an ethnic, natural, and "rootsy" feel dominated the first few years of the 1970s as people explored New Age thinking and cheaper air travel made it possible to visit far-flung places. The hippie fashions from the previous decade were reworked with a folksy vibe, taking traditional crafts such as knitting, needlepoint, weaving, and dyeing to the very epicenter of fashion. Britain continued to produce many innovative designers. The art deco revival, triggered by the work of Royal College of Art lecturer Bernard Nevill for Liberty, flourished. New inspiration was born through collaborations of fashion and art in the work of designers such as Ossie Clark and Celia Birtwell, Bill Gibb, and Zandra Rhodes. Malcolm McLaren sold 1950s memorabilia at his Let It Rock shop before pulling the plug on the whole retro trend in 1974 and opening a new shop called simply SEX. In 1977, he and partner Vivienne Westwood renamed their shop Seditionaries. At the other end of the spectrum from the outrageous Westwood, Jean Muir was creating elegantly restrained clothes in jersey and suede. Elsewhere, top-quality ready-to-wear fashion established a solid base, with Givenchy, Oscar de la Renta, Yves Saint Laurent, Marc Bohan for Dior, and Karl Lagerfeld for Chloé wholesaling around the world. In the United States, Calvin Klein, Geoffrey Beene, Ralph Lauren, and others created new, flowing jersey separates and easy-to-wear classics for working women. Diane von Furstenberg's signature wraparound dress was a huge hit, and New York's Studio 54 became the most famous discotheque in the world.

1970s

Clothes with an ethnic, natural, and "rootsy" feel dominated the first few years of the 1970s as people explored New Age thinking and cheaper air travel made it possible to visit far-flung places. The hippie fashions from the previous decade were reworked with a folksy vibe, taking traditional crafts such as knitting, needlepoint, weaving, and dyeing to the very epicenter of fashion. Britain continued to produce many innovative designers. The art deco revival, triggered by the work of Royal College of Art lecturer Bernard Nevill for Liberty, flourished. New inspiration was born through collaborations of fashion and art in the work of designers such as Ossie Clark and Celia Birtwell, Bill Gibb, and Zandra Rhodes. Malcolm McLaren sold 1950s memorabilia at his Let It Rock shop before pulling the plug on the whole retro trend in 1974 and opening a new shop called simply SEX. In 1977, he and partner Vivienne Westwood renamed their shop Seditionaries. At the other end of the spectrum from the outrageous Westwood, Jean Muir was creating elegantly restrained clothes in jersey and suede. Elsewhere, top-quality ready-to-wear fashion established a solid base, with Givenchy, Oscar de la Renta, Yves Saint Laurent, Marc Bohan for Dior, and Karl Lagerfeld for Chloé wholesaling around the world. In the United States, Calvin Klein, Geoffrey Beene, Ralph Lauren, and others created new, flowing jersey separates and easy-to-wear classics for working women. Diane von Furstenberg's signature wraparound dress was a huge hit, and New York's Studio 54 became the most famous discotheque in the world.

Daywear

It's easy to get lost in the drama of 1970s fashion and forget that this was the decade in which ready-to-wear came into its own. Separates were a key component, instead of whole outfits in the formal couture sense. Fashion editors showed women how to wear them, pulling together different patterns and fabrics with a couple of key colors. "Together but apart" was fashion's most wearable message yet.

The new luxury ready-to-wear began in the 1960s, when a few designers broke away from the rigid, expensive traditions of couture and began producing easy-to-purchase lines to be sold in their own shops. Oscar de la Renta opened his first ready-to-wear boutique in 1965, with Yves Saint Laurent following in 1966 and Hubert de Givenchy in 1968. By 1970, such shops were forming the cornerstones of the modern fashion industry, making designer clothes accessible to all who could afford them.

Yves Saint Laurent's collections

In the 1970s, Saint Laurent's influence became widespread with his partnership with Pierre Bergé, who not only gave him the freedom to design with less financial restraint but also aided him in his expansion from haute couture to ready-to-wear. His 1971 collection, 1940, showed gangster-style pantsuits with double-breasted jackets. Square shoulders, bouffant sleeves, and a green fox-fur jacket led this 1940s innovation to have a huge effect on daywear, which carried on until 1973, with black silk two-pieces and dresses of silk crepe de chine featuring simple white floral patterns, short puffed sleeves, nipped-in waists, and rounded collars. Similar styles were created by Karl Lagerfeld for Chloé, by Cacharel, and by Ossie Clark.

Saint Laurent had always loved to marry fashion with art, and as the decade continued, he created more adventurous looks harking back to his revolutionary designs of the 1960s, influenced by op art and Mondrian. In 1979 his "Homage to Picasso" collection featured strong graphic prints on wool, gabardine, and satin. Yet such collections were balanced by his ready-to-wear classics. A strongly wearable nautical collection of sailor-wide linen trousers, knitted sailor tops, and bolero jackets in the mid-1970s was followed by his Russian Ballet Opera collection in 1976 and a Mongolian-inspired wool, fur, and knitwear collection for fall/winter 1977.

PAGE 144 Nicky Samuel, 1970s It Girl, wearing a Tulip dress by Celia Birtwell, 1971, for a *Vogue* shoot.

OPPOSITE Early 1970s
lips-print dress by Yves
Saint Laurent for his
ready-to-wear line,
Rive Gauche.

RIGHT Two pantsuits from
the American label R & K
Originals, 1970, are wool
knit-polyester blends.
The overlong tunic top
and wide lapels were
typical details of 1970s
ready-to-wear.

"Le Smoking," the women's tuxedo introduced by Saint Laurent in the 1960s (see also page 121) and reworked in the 1970s, heralded the arrival of the decade's mainstay, the pantsuit, which reflected the trend for all things unisex. Pretty soon, versions were available in wool plaids and tweeds, with satin and velvet for evenings, and boutiques and department stores were selling cheaper alternatives in such fabrics as acrylic and polyester to eager customers.

Fluidity and comfort in fashion

While the Parisian fashion houses offered luxurious, even flamboyant, daywear shapes in fabrics including cotton drill, felt, heavy wools, crepe, and fur, another silhouette took shape. After the shift dresses and hard lines of the 1960s, more feminine clothes reemerged, following the shape of the female form with fluidity and movement. Soft, flattering wool jersey fabrics fitted and flared away from the body, creating a new, less restricted silhouette. Jean Muir lowered hemlines after the mini left fashion with nowhere to go, and the midi was reborn. In 1973 the H-shape brought a low waist and longer hem.

Other Jean Muir designs also caused a stir, keeping this designer at the cutting edge of style. Jersey culottes and tunics, leather-trimmed jumpers, and trademark turtlenecks were clothes with a message. Eschewing pretty, sexy, and playful, Muir's customers were not afraid to be bold, stylish, and vocal. She moved on from her 1960s label, Jane & Jane, to her own eponymous label in 1966; her muse, British actress Joanna Lumley, had been a 1960s babe, but she chopped off her hair, darkened her lips, and reworked her look to match Muir's trademark dark palette of black, navy, and chocolate brown.

Ease and comfort combined with style were the key elements of these clothes, worn over the latest designs in underwear. Balcony bras, corseted waists, and complicated garter/stocking combinations had died out with the previous decade, giving way to more comfortable, less structured garments in elasticized fabrics with natural shaping. The aim, said the fashion magazines of the time, was to look as though you were not wearing any underwear at all.

American style

Meanwhile, fledgling New York designers, including Ralph Lauren and Calvin Klein, were infusing their city with new fashion excitement. Together with Geoffrey Beene, their classic tailoring with a flourish – including luxurious camel-hair coats by Calvin Klein in 1971 – were the building blocks of what was to become the easy, sporty American style, carried through by such fashion models as Lauren Hutton, Patti Hansen, and Margaux Hemingway. This was daywear on a far simpler scale than that of the Europeans, in soft, neutral colors with natural accessories.

Ralph Lauren took American history as his theme and moved on from the slick daywear and sportswear of his peers to create casual chic. Preppy slacks, polo shirts, and simple sweaters were reminiscent of Princeton in the 1920s; later, Western and Native American influences brought a new glamour to casual clothes. Lauren's designs, worn by Robert Redford in the 1974 film *The Great Gatsby,* based on F. Scott Fitzgerald's novel, gave international exposure to American fashions of the 1920s as worn by the rich of that day. His classic designs for the Polo line said "no work today," yet denoted the wearer to be a person of means and substance.

Perhaps the most influential look Lauren created was seen on Diane Keaton in Woody Allen's 1977 film *Annie Hall.* Lauren had already begun reworking menswear classics for women, but Keaton brought the look to life on screen. Tailored raincoats, men's shirts, jackets, and trousers were accessorized with cinched-in belts and hats. Wide belts, ties, kooky sunglasses, and fun shoes softened the masculine separates.

Geoffrey Beene and Calvin Klein also created softer versions of masculine styling for the women's market. Both started out by specializing in casual sportswear (a term for comfortable, informal clothes – not to be confused with "active sportswear," such as tracksuits or hiking clothes). Klein has been quoted as saying, "I like clothes that slide when the body moves." Soft jerseys, fleece fabrics, and easy cotton separates were part of this look; and Beene was one of the first designers to use fine synthetic fabrics for his trademark, easy designs. In 1974 the Beene Bag dress was hugely popular, a dress essentially made of two pieces of fabric with holes for hands and neck, which draped beautifully in at the knees, fitting anyone who tried it.

Geoffrey Beene pioneered the softly draped jersey dress, which appeared in many forms in the 1970s in collections by other great Americans, including Roy Halston and Bill Blass. Yet all their versions were overshadowed by the most famous dress of all time, Diane von Furstenberg's wrap dress. In 1972, Belgian-born fashion designer Diane von Furstenberg arrived in New York; a year later, she produced her first line of the wrap dress. It was perfect for the times. Working women were emerging as a force to be reckoned with in the U.S., and it became possible for a woman to be sexy, attractive, and successful all at the same time. American working women loved the professional yet feminine style of the wrap dress. Three years later, this drip-dry cotton jersey garment, cut to flatter and available in a number of natural wood-block prints, had sold 5 million copies. The DVF brand was born. "Feel like a woman, wear a dress!" became von Furstenberg's trademark phrase. Relaunched in the 1990s, von Furstenberg's name once again became synonymous with grown-up feminine chic.

ABOVE AND OPPOSITE LEFT Brown wool early-1970s suit by British boutique label Biba. The trouser suit gained prominence in the 1970s, here with wide pant legs and cuffs. The amazing optical effect of the weave can be seen in detail, above.

OPPOSITE RIGHT Jean Muir gray pinafore dress with leather trim, early 1970s, a fine example of her sharp tailoring skills and the immaculate precision of her designs. She was known for her ability to work jersey, leather, wool, and cashmere into fluid but perfectly proportioned shapes.

Back-to-Nature Fashions

OPPOSITE Marisa Berenson, American actress, model, and granddaughter of Elsa Schiaparelli, in a geometric wrap dress by Sibley Coffee, 1970. Design influences from such far-flung hippie trails as India and Morocco found their way into prints and textiles during the 1970s.

The rebellious political mood of the 1960s spilled over into fashion. By 1970 nobody wanted to dress like their parents, and there was a reaction against the mass production of food and fashion among the politically aware. Back to Nature was the slogan, along with renewed interest in fantasy, magic, and the spirit. The Beatles had been to India, sparking the popularity of yoga and Eastern concepts of spiritual development. Morocco became a vacation destination for rich hippies like Talitha Getty and designers such as Ossie Clark and Yves Saint Laurent.

Wearing the clothes of ethnic cultures that lived closer to nature was equated with freedom from the bonds of Western life – somehow people felt closer to Mother Earth in the naturally dyed heavy cottons or cheesecloth of India or the colorful, striped knitwear of Peru. Embellished fabrics from Greece, Turkey, and farther into Arabia, featuring mirrors, beading, bells, and intricate embroidery, were hot. Styling details including layers, toggle fastenings, ponchos, and shawls as accessories, rickrack, and embroidered purses on long cord or string worn across the body all added to the look. Eclecticism was the mark of the rich hippie: She still wore furs, but not the traditional, unfashionable Fifth Avenue mink. Instead, she went for floor-length white Afghan lambskin or patchwork rabbit creations from gypsy dealers and junk markets.

The folk look drifted across the Atlantic from the United States, where the hippie movement had been born in the 1960s. Bob Dylan, the Byrds, the Mamas & Papas and Joni Mitchell were all proponents of rock-folk fusion and its fashion offshoots. In Europe, the mood was more political. Hippie-folk vibes were alive and kicking in Amsterdam after John Lennon and Yoko Ono spent their much-publicized honeymoon in the Amsterdam Hilton in 1969. In Paris, Sonia Rykiel produced folkish bag-belts, echoing the peasant feel of the moment. She along with Dorothée Bis also began creating funky knitwear, aimed at young feisty Parisians, still sore from the student riots of the 1960s.

British designers

London's Portobello Road market became a magnet for those seeking the ethnic look, as stallholders diversified from antiques and junk into ethnic bric-a-brac and clothing. Canny boutique owners also saw a gap in the fashion market. Thea Porter imported Middle Eastern artifacts into her shop on Greek Street, London, and produced a series of unique garments heavily influenced by her childhood years spent in prewar Beirut. Like Zandra Rhodes, she produced her own prints in cottons and silks, sewing together different, vivid panels of clashing colors in flamboyant, Eastern-inspired designs. Porter can take the credit for putting the caftan on the fashion map; this garment was rapidly adopted by such stars as Elizabeth Taylor and Barbra Streisand on the lookout for a touch of bohemia.

One of the key British designers of the decade was Bill Gibb, a farmer's son from Scotland, who was named *Vogue* designer of the year in 1970. A lover of fantasy, he based his collections around natural themes like the forest floor or mountains and sea. Wild, colorful prints clashed in the same garments, coupled with nostalgic medieval styling. Long sleeves, tight bodices, scoop necks, lacings, ribbons, and overskirts all featured in his designs, made up in silks, chiffon, and cotton. A typical Gibb evening dress from 1971, in his own hand-printed silk blues and reds, had huge double-gathered sleeves, a peplum waist, full skirt and asymmetrical braid around collar, cuffs, panels, and hems, contrasting with two different print patterns on skirt, and sleeves.

As the 1970s evolved, elements of traditional Indian, Mexican, Russian, and Eastern European dress made it into all the big collections. Zandra Rhodes's early designs were inspired by ethnic cultures as diverse as those of Ukrainian peasants and Native Americans. Her Chevron shawl design drew inspiration from the quilting and stitching of the Russian steppes, which she found in a picture book. Quilted on unbleached muslin, Rhodes's circular coat with zigzag hem summed up her amazing work at this time. Two years later, Rhodes's classic show at the Roundhouse, London, in 1972 – with designs inspired by Native American culture and

RIGHT American actress Ali MacGraw exhibits the decade's ethnic and crafts-oriented influences in her dress: a flowered blouse and skirt by Patti Cappalli for Addenda with a black macramé vest, macramé belt, beaded head wrap by Maharajah of India, and lace-up boots by Latinas. Taken in 1970, the photograph is highly reminiscent of Native American portraits with the headdress and direct gaze to the camera.

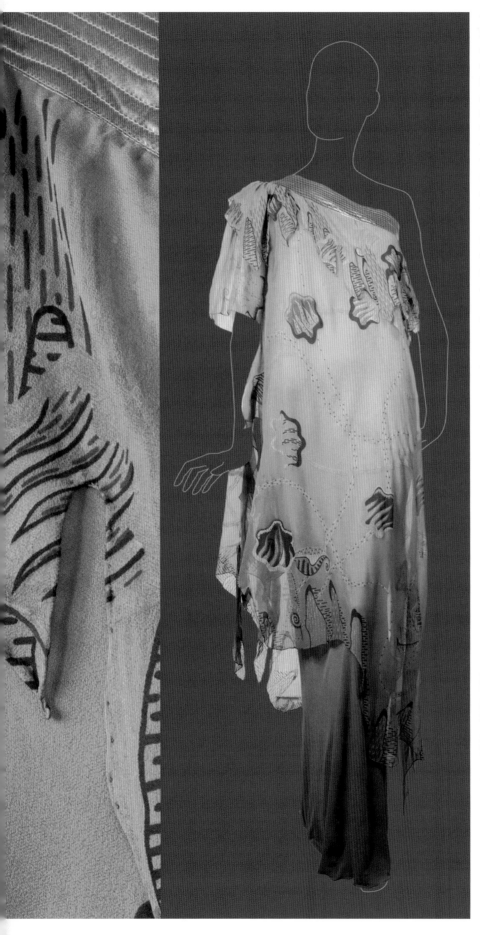

featuring lightweight feather prints with string and bead detailing in muted natural blues, rusts, creams, and black – put her on the fashion map. Her delightful printed designs, including the famous Butterflies series, cut into flattering silk slimline ensembles, and shifts or billowing chiffon creations, remained her mainstays until 1977. However, as punk took hold, she decided that her butterflies felt too fragile for the changing climate, and she created her first dresses in plain black or shocking-pink silk jersey. In these, ripped and pinned with chains, "street" and couture crossed paths again, and Rhodes was dubbed the Priestess of Punk (see also pages 172–3).

Ethnic and natural trends also paved the way for innovative print designers who took their inspiration from nature. Celia Birtwell's flower-inspired fabrics became fashionable, their bold, swirling patterns contrasting with the pretty traditional florals sold by Laura Ashley. Soon a crop of designers would emerge who would take all these elements and bring something new to the picture. Textile print designers Veronica Marsh and Althea McNish created bold, colorful designs for a new generation of buyers in Britain.

International designers

Meanwhile, in the United States, Patti Cappalli's range for Addenda spread the same vibrant new agenda. Pablo and Delia, two designers who arrived in London from Argentina, created fantasy-based prints for evening gowns. By 1973, they had set themselves up as London's coolest design couple, and they enjoyed a brief stay at the top of the arts-inspired fashion movement. The pair branched out into daywear, creating jumpers, blouses, and wearable separates before their eventual demise as a design partnership in the late 1970s (though Delia Cancela went on to become a respected artist in Argentina). Meanwhile, on the Continent, mainstream designers dabbled with looks inspired by the fantasists, but they were still shaking off the hard lines of couture.

SIGNATURE ZANDRA RHODES ELEMENTS:

- ❖ Asymmetrical hems and necklines
- ❖ Circular cutting on coats and capes
- ❖ Cactus, shell, and butterfly designs
- ❖ Feather adornment
- ❖ Handkerchief and cut-into hemlines
- ❖ Caftan shapes
- ❖ Multilayered chiffon
- ❖ Conceptual Chic silk jersey evening dresses with ripped-out holes, safety pin, and chain detailing
- ❖ Vibrant colors

ABOVE AND OPPOSITE Gray-and-pink chiffon one-shoulder Zandra Rhodes dress over jersey lining with quilted satin band and slashed hand-rolled edges, 1974, with label detail.

RIGHT Zandra Rhodes's groundbreaking Chevron Shawl print on an unbleached muslin quilted coat, 1970.

ABOVE AND RIGHT A craftsman costumer, Bill Gibb merged embroidery, slashed sleeves, satin, and prints together in his truly imaginative hippie-style dresses. With its incredible decoration and details, worked across a voluminous surface of fabric, the overall print of this 1970 Bill Gibb dress reads like an Italian marbled-paper masterpiece.

OPPOSITE Under deep pleated layers, the sleeve is secured with hidden buttons along an interior panel of fabric in an alternative print.

Ossie Clark and Celia Birtwell

The bohemian flavor of the 1970s, in which art and fashion amalgamated beautifully, was nowhere more apparent than in the work of British designer Ossie Clark and his wife, Celia Birtwell, whom he married in 1969. Born in Liverpool but dubbed "Ossie" because he had spent time in Oswaldtwhistle, in Lancashire, as an evacuee toddler during the Second World War, Clark graduated from the Royal College of Art in 1965. He became a cult figure on London's fashion scene; during his peak, between 1968 and 1974, each new collection of essentially similar garments was heralded by *Vogue* and the fashion media as "groundbreaking."

As Clark's success increased, his circle of friends grew to encompass artists like David Hockney and Patrick Proctor and rock stars such as Bryan Ferry and the Rolling Stones – in 1972-3 Clark designed Mick Jagger's stage catsuits. His early shows, featuring favorite models Patti Boyd, Patti D'Arbanville, Gala Mitchell, and transsexual Amanda Lear, were true rock 'n' roll events. Parading the catwalk at Chelsea Town Hall in 1970 and the Royal Court Theatre in 1971, the models "did their own thing," revealing a wild glamour that epitomized Ossie's philosophy of classic with a definite twist.

Clark's skill lay in his ability to cut and shape fabric around the female form with a subtle extravagance that was sexy and chic. He pioneered the midi and maxi lengths in the late 1960s, where other design houses, including Dior, had failed. Until their divorce in 1974, Clark and Birtwell created their designs for Quorum, the Chelsea fashion boutique owned by Alice Pollock, a designer whose mini-fashion empire was the hub of swinging London. Birtwell's print designs came to life in her husband's chiffon pantsuits of 1970. Cream, with swirling art deco-inspired plant and flower patterns on

ABOVE AND LEFT Ossie Clark dress with Celia Birtwell floral print, 1972. The bias-cut length hugs the body, while the back ties secure the sleeves and neckline.

SIGNATURE OSSIE CLARK ELEMENTS:

- ❖ Rounded or pointed collars, or deep V-necks
- ❖ Bias cutting
- ❖ Fitted peplum jackets
- ❖ Tulip-shaped skirts
- ❖ Maxi coats
- ❖ Ruffles
- ❖ Puffed-out sleeves between narrow shoulders and narrow cuffs
- ❖ Chiffon pantsuits
- ❖ Gently fitted shapes
- ❖ Layering; e.g., shorter sleeves over long, or minidresses over pants

the wide sleeves and the skirt of the mini-overdress, and around the hems of flared trousers, this was daywear of the prettiest kind. Clark would incorporate her floral prints in evening dresses, alternating swathes of contrasting prints in a bias-cut, floor-length satin or crepe de chine spiral.

Alongside his coveted dresses, Clark's tailoring was equally desirable. Totally new ideas, like floral-printed wool fashioned into a beautiful fitted winter coat, inspired a whole generation of copies. Among other pieces were three-piece pantsuits in Birtwell-print velvet and zipped bomber jackets in patent python skin or similar three-buttoned, closely fitted versions in black, brown, navy, or deep red. There are few Ossie Clark originals to be found in the modern vintage market. Most of the garments he made for his London clients (including Nicky Samuel – wife of Nigel Weymouth, owner of 1970s boutique Granny Takes A Trip – and Alfred Radley, whose family business backed

Clark and Quorum financially) have stayed in their family's private collections, or they have simply been worn out by their lucky owners. There were copies around, but Clark's style was too perfectionist for many to be able to mimic it adequately. He revived the bias-cut dress after picking up 1930s originals in Portobello Market during the 1960s and taking them home to experiment with. The bias became one of his signature shapes – the flexibility and slight stretchiness of bias cuts on fine fabrics like crepe de chine enable them to fit in the most flattering way. Although Clark's designs favored large-breasted body shapes with narrow hips, his clothes flattered anyone who could fit into them comfortably. After their divorce, the couple went their separate ways, and there is no denying the loss to British fashion of this dynamic duo's joint creative powers. Hardworking, dedicated Birtwell continues to design today and deserves state recognition – a damehood at least – for her services to British fashion.

ABOVE Ossie Clark with friend and collaborator Alice Pollock of Quorum in a photograph by Lord Snowdon.

LEFT Front and back views of a 1971 Ossie Clark–Celia Birtwell coat with puffed sleeves, pointed lapels, and Birtwell's famous Floating Daisy print. With its tie-front fastening, the coat was made to be worn over a coordinating dress in the same colorway.

OPPOSITE A variation of the Floating Daisy design in another Clark–Birtwell coat, this time featuring the floral print alongside a grid design on the bodice, rounded collar, and sleeves. The buttons intersect the grid neatly down the bodice.

BELOW, TOP Celia Birtwell's Floating Daisy pattern. Clusters of dark-eyed flowers are linked by stripy stems in a curving pattern that reflected Ossie Clark's form-fitting bias cut to the dress.

BELOW, BOTTOM This floral print mingles poppies with trailing stems. Here, the motifs appear in red and blue on a cream ground. Other typical Birtwell motifs included geometrics, leaves, fruits, and stars.

BELOW, TOP This exotic print is typically exuberantly Birtwell – a mix of graphic and natural motifs – stripes, waves, palm leaves, and cloverlike trails in blue and black on a lemon-yellow field.

BELOW, BOTTOM Oversized blue flowers on a long coat make a high-impact statement. Birtwell's textiles were inspired by nature: scattered lilies and tulips, trailing leaves, and stems.

OPPOSITE A 1974 advertisement for an Ossie Clark dress with a Birtwell print, by Jim Lee. The designs are as wearable and covetable today as they were in the 1970s.

ABOVE Ossie Clark jacket, 1970, combining several Birtwell prints. The curved front pockets accentuate the feminine hourglass silhouette. Exquisite tailoring was an Ossie trademark, along with workmanship worthy of Parisian couture. The flat-lying lapels and V-neck accentuated the breasts.

BELOW An Ossie Clark yellow fringed pantsuit with knickers, 1971. Despite the slightly Western styling, the fabric is crepe, and the print is by Celia Birtwell. The strong colors, graphic print, and ornate styling of the piece gives it a bold, dramatic presence.

Decorative Arts and Crafts Revivals

In the 1970s, organic farming and self-sufficiency thrived alongside a revival of interest in traditional handicrafts. Evening classes in knitting, macramé, embroidery, weaving, and pottery began to appear. Detail became a crucial element of fashion, emerging all the way through the decade in different ways, from hand-crafted knitted, woven, and embroidered fabrics to patchwork and pleating mid-decade, followed by another appliqué revival at the end of the decade.

Several designers of the 1970s were noted for their interest in reviving traditional craftsmanship. In Britain, Laura Ashley's early designs were inspired by country crafts; yokes, smocking, embroidery, brocade, and lace details set her clothes apart from more mass-produced versions. They helped to supply a growing market for traditional and even Victorian-style clothes.

Bill Gibb used wool, reworking such traditional knits as Fair Isle and Arran into different patterns and weaves with new properties. He put knitted vests over evening dresses and gave the whole concept of knitting a new image. Crochet, nubby textures, beading, and unusually small or large stitches came to characterize his work, as more designers followed his lead and began to work with knitted fabrics. Gibb also liked to take traditional Scottish woven fabrics, including tweed, and give them a new twist. One of his 1970 designs features a heavily patterned pigskin jacket worn over a knife-pleated, checked tweed skirt. Although Gibb teamed up with American knitwear designer Kaffe Fassett on several occasions in joint ventures, he was destined never to capitalize on his creativity, owing to constant financial difficulties.

Knitted fabrics were not just craft-inspired, folksy, and ethnic-looking. Since the 1960s, designers including Sonia Rykiel and Missoni had been fashioning garments from stretchy knits. By the early 1970s such looks were big fashion news at other major houses, including Krizia. Missoni's trademark zigzag, finely striped multicolor knits helped to establish it as Milan's biggest fashion company, planting the northern Italian city firmly on the fashion map. Meanwhile, British names like Jeff Banks and Daniel Hechter entered the market with stylish knitted tank tops and V-necked, deep-ribbed, cuff-sleeved sweaters. The tabard-style overtop – a wide-sleeved, long-lined tunic, often belted at the waist and worn over a turtleneck sweater – was big news in 1976. Farther down the fashion chain, knitwear became popular in department and chain stores, with cheaper brands producing sporty hotpants, vests, leggings, and leg warmers in acrylic yarn.

LEFT Missoni 1970s top and fringed overshirt. The exceptional colors and textures have made Missoni pieces highly collectible and as popular today as when first produced by sisters Tai and Rosita Missoni in 1953. Worldwide attention started in the late 1960s, and the 1970s saw them producing dresses, coats, skirts, and pants, as well as sweaters.

OPPOSITE The back view of a 1979 knitted coat by Kaffe Fassett, who was known for his rich, many-colored palette and geometric patterns. The muted colors and full sleeves, which draw on Renaissance and Eastern dress, show his influential creative skills. The colors and shape also recall the work of Missoni and Bill Gibb; indeed, Fassett's early collections were commissioned by both.

ABOVE AND LEFT Late-1970s kimono-style orange Bill Gibb coat, with label detail, above. Gibb caught the decade's predilection for ethnic clothes and, like many designers of the time, was inspired by European and Eastern folk costumes, particularly in his ingenious use of textures, weaves, and patterns. The sheer scale of his garments made his designs bold and larger than life – like many of the individuals who wore them.

BELOW Bill Gibb's amazing surface decoration is shown here in this close-up from an intricately quilted and appliquéd orange silk evening suit with butterflies, 1970. This attention to detail won him the moniker Master of the Decorative.

RIGHT Late-1970s Bill Gibb cape with border and fill geometric patterns, which enhance the sweeping drama of the piece's shape.

LEFT Brown Bill Gibb leather coat, 1972, with finely embroidered and screen-printed silver bees and chrysanthemums. By the mid-1970s Gibb was working with leather, especially in coats and jackets with wide collars and peplums.

Japanese Visionaries

Although Japanese fashion had been traditional for centuries, the dawn of the techno-revolution sparked design interest in all things cultural, and by the early 1970s new design names began to emerge. Fashion was the natural medium for the inspired creativity of Kansai Yamamoto, Issey Miyake, and Kenzo Takada, and later Hanae Mori, Yohji Yamamoto, and Rei Kawakubo of Comme des Garçons. Described as funny and quirky by fashion journalists, their work undoubtedly introduced an element of fun as well as some amazing styling.

Issey Miyake's early designs show his genius with fabric, as in his red silk print evening dress with sash waist and layers of fabric, which seemed to show no traditional fastenings at all. The broad spectrum of his inventiveness was demonstrated in one fashion shoot that had models wearing – among other outfits – thigh-high red suede boots with wraparound ties over checkerboard leggings with a matching jacket in red and white, and multicolored, three-way striped combinations topped with a matching miniskirt in greens, blues, and reds.

Kansai Yamamoto took elements from traditional Kabuki theater costume, including a giant red mask, which he printed onto modern kimonos, T-shirts, and knitwear. After his first London design house was opened in 1971, his clothes were quickly snatched up by the fashion cognoscenti, eager for yet another take on the vogue for all things Eastern and ethnic.

A Japanese fashion explosion followed, and no one epitomized this look better than model Marie Helvin or Yoko Ono. As the oriental influence on fashion took hold, the designers themselves branched out. Kenzo Takada began his career with a Paris boutique – Jungle Jap, so called after the jungle patterns and prints of which he was so fond. Starting with simple smocks, wide-legged trousers, wraparound skirts, and long tops in plain, dark-colored cottons or padded fabrics, he went on to produce pretty western-style floral prints with Victorian design details, including pinned and tucked bodices and billowing petticoat and skirt ensembles, which were in keeping with the vintage fashion feel of the early 1970s. Later, as knitwear became a key medium, Kenzo introduced his signature stripy knits. Layering the knits over each other, he created an easy-to-wear trend and was the first to show a bulky sweater over a short miniskirt with a belt at the hips, creating an enduring, youthful fashion shape that has transcended time.

Quilting was also a distinctive element of the work of many of the Japanese designers, including Kansai Yamamoto, whose 1972 spring collection featured a green quilted velvet pantsuit with cropped flares and a silver quilted raincoat with matching hat.

OPPOSITE Artist and political activist Caroline Coon models a red-and-white, handknitted, woolen jumpsuit by Japanese designer Kansai Yamamoto, 1971, featuring his Kabuki theater mask.

BELOW Shirtdress in a navy-and-white Japanese-inspired print by Hanae Mori, with a twined rope belt by Yves Saint Laurent, and a purple suede watch cap by Mr. John, 1970. Mori established her haute couture collection and fashion house in Paris in 1977, becoming known for her restrained elegance and delicacy.

Punk Fashions

Invented in Britain by Malcolm McLaren and Vivienne Westwood, punk fashion certainly came as a surprise to everyone. It started out as extreme bondage gear sold in SEX, the King's Road emporium that the pair later relabeled Seditionaries. The overall look, as sold by McLaren and Westwood, combined the traditional components of bondage gear, including rubber, leather, studs, straps, and buckles, with other elements. Muslin and cotton T-shirts, shirts, narrow trousers, and undershirts were ripped up and then pinned back together again to form loose, layered garments. Skintight leather jeans, mini-kilts, dyed cotton drill trousers with the legs joined together with straps formed the foundation of the punk outfit. The biker jacket, the classic teenage garment of rebellion, was also part of the style, but this time in red patent leather or pink plastic.

Punk separated street fashion from the elitist, higher end of the market for good. The fashion press just did not get it and labeled the punks trash. Punk rock was as much a part of the fashion movement as the clothes, characterized by the same anarchic subversion and anti-Establishment stance, although the music itself soon evolved into New Wave, then fizzled out into a mélange of different sounds.

Punk fashion revolutionized the way people dressed, kicking off a number of trends with far-reaching influences. Until 1977, trousers had been steadily flaring outward, reaching anything up to 20 inches wide. By the fall of that year, the punks were wearing drainpipe jeans – industrial Wranglers and Levis that they had customized themselves. This in itself was almost as shocking for many as the safety pins, snot, and swearing. To balance the new skinny-leg shapes brought in by punk, shoulders were padded out and built up. These changes spread into mainstream fashion, and by 1978 straight-leg trousers were everywhere, and padded shoulders and longer-line jackets featured in collections by Marc Bohan at Dior, Adrian Cartmel for Manson, Yves Saint Laurent's Rive Gauche, and Genny at Regine.

For a brief moment, street trends and fashion met up on the disco dance floor. Inspired by the safety pins, buckles, and badges of punk, Karl Lagerfeld created big, star-shaped pins and brooches for Chloé. Throughout the 1970s, Lagerfeld's designs stayed closest of all the designers' to the street in terms of trends. His youthful touch and intrinsic understanding of the fashion zeitgeist kept him on track and slightly apart from the haughtier couturiers. Marc Bohan at Dior also designed with a youthful trendy touch, clearly influenced by the shapes and colors of punk.

In fact, punk gave couture a new direction. Strong colors, including bright pink and red, and plaids inspired by tartans appeared in the late 1970s collections of the major houses. When Marc Bohan finally left Dior in 1992, it was felt that a new spirit was needed at the classic fashion house, but during the late 1970s Bohan was truly the master of sexy funky chic on the international fashion circuit. Back then, Dior developed a slick glamour, reinvented later in the 1990s by John Galliano. A quick flick through the pages of *Vogue* from the late 1970s reveals the divide between mainstream couture fashion and the funkier, punkier, nighttime dressing inspired by punk.

Zandra Rhodes' Conceptual Chic look, featuring punk-style evening gowns ripped and torn to shreds, capitalized on the feeling of division that was everywhere in popular culture postpunk. Meanwhile, future design talents were preparing for their own onslaught, which came in the 1980s, when, thanks to government recognition and fashion pioneers such as public relations master Lynne Franks, British fashion came into its own. Betty Jackson worked for Radley (though Ossie Clark, their chief designer at the time, reputedly refused to speak to her), Katharine Hamnett was designing jeans for Tuttabankem, and Antony Price created looks for the chain store Stirling Cooper. All these names and more would emerge, with their own directional, groundbreaking looks, in the 10 years after punk.

ABOVE AND BELOW Vivienne Westwood dog-collar knit for the Let It Rock label, from the 1971 Let It Rock shop, which was supplanted in name by Too Fast To Live, Too Young To Die in 1972, SEX in 1974, Seditionaries in 1977, and World's End from 1980. In the beginning Let It Rock focused on 1950s revival pieces, but as this piece from the period shows, Westwood's and McLaren's subversive turn toward punk was fast approaching.

ABOVE AND RIGHT Westwood's clothes from her 1976 Bondage collection were studded, buckled, strapped, chained, and zippered. The BOY bondage trousers, label above and pictured right, are an exact copy of Westwood's Seditionaries originals. BOY bought the rights to sell a limited range from Westwood and McLaren from 1976 until the early 1980s. The Cambridge Rapist T-shirt is from the SEX label, 1976.

LEFT Black-and-white Hangman pullover by Westwood and McLaren's Seditionaries label, 1977. Reminiscent of a straightjacket with the overlong arms, the "noose" neck-fastening loops around to enclose the collar. The chaotic, uneven texture of the knit and the noose-tie shape were details that greatly influenced the work of other designers.

OPPOSITE Detail from a Zandra Rhodes Conceptual Chic dress, 1977, in black rayon jersey. Its punk styling is evidenced in the asymmetrical holes, beaded safety pins, ball-link chains, and diamanté decoration.

Denim and Leather

**"Blue jean baby, LA lady, seamstress for the band,"
sang Elton John in his 1971 song "Tiny Dancer,"
based on Maxine Taupin, wife of his songwriting
partner Bernie. The words epitomized the modern
idea of jeans as the sexy casual uniform of the rock
'n' roll elite.** Denim had crept up on fashion in the
1960s, with Yves Saint Laurent creating cool brushed-
denim pantsuits. The great designer was later to lament
that his one regret on looking back over his career was
that he "did not invent the blue jean." Naturally, other
designers cashed in. Soon there were top-end purveyors
including Fiorucci, whose stores in Europe and the
United States sold a glamorous, Continental denim style
as sported on the beaches of San Tropez. In London,
Katherine Hamnett began designing kooky hotpants
and denim mini ensembles for the label Tuttabankem.
Until the late 1970s, when denim suddenly went upscale,
patchwork, studded, paneled, bleached, and fringed
leather and denim styles interwove to create a unisex
look that increased in flamboyance.

The Americans, who invented denim jeans during
the middle of the nineteenth century courtesy of
Levi Strauss, came up with designer jeans aimed
specifically at women looking for the perfect fit. First
came Gloria Vanderbilt's version in 1978, with its swan
insignia and diamanté sparkle. Vanderbilt jeans were
cut like fitted straight-legged women's trousers and
were supposedly of better quality than ordinary
versions. Female shoppers went for the designer jeans
concept in droves. Although Vanderbilt jeans did not
stay cool for long, their legacy spawned the huge
industry that lives on today. In 1979, when 15-year-old
starlet Brooke Shields told the world, "You know what
comes between me and my Calvins? Nothing," the label
jean had arrived. The Calvin Klein jeans modeled by
Shields were high-waisted and straight-legged, tapering
in slightly at the ankle.

In 1970, Roberto Cavalli set up shop selling a small
range of sexy leather separates. Soon leather vests,
jackets, skirts, and pants became as cool as denim.
When denim went designer, the leather jacket was
quickly snatched up and reworked by Thierry Mugler and
Claude Montana. Karl Lagerfeld at Chloé also helped to
put leather on the designer map. Mugler's fall 1978
collection featured a white velvet, diamanté-studded
jumpsuit and bronze leather jackets, which had studded
diagonal fastenings, astronaut padding details, and
matching skullcaps. Meanwhile, Jap (Kenzo Takada's line)
delivered pink leather tuxedos. By 1979 soft pigskin and
suede were trademark tailoring materials in collections
by Maxfield Parrish, Bruce Oldfield, and Nicole Fahri for
Stephen Marks. Fahri's punched suede blazer in beige,
with narrow lapels and soft gathered and padded
shoulders, tapped into the decade's love of suede.

ABOVE Tuttabankem
leather appliqué hotpants
and vest, 1970-1.
Tuttabankem was cofounded
in 1970 by Katherine
Hamnett and Anne Buck,
who sold their pieces to
Henri Bendel, Saks, Browns,
and Alexander's of Rome
before Hamnett launched
her own label in 1975.

OPPOSITE Russian model
Veruschka in the Borghese
Gardens in Rome, wearing
a light suede vest and
shorts with a dark shirt
and leather belts by Gucci,
with knee-high black leather
boots by Valentino, 1971.

Glam-Rock Influences

Glam, or glitter, rock dominated the music charts from 1973 to 1975, but the sparkly stage costumes went unnoticed until the real trendsetters – David Bowie, Roxy Music, and T-Rex in Britain, and Alice Cooper, Iggy Pop, and New York Dolls in the U.S. – came on the scene. Rock revolutionaries in tights, wigs, and makeup, they were the musical and visual antidote to the hairy monsters of heavy rock, mixing rock music with art, cross-dressing with heterosexuality, debauchery with elegance. Former art students and, in the case of Roxy Music's Bryan Ferry, a teacher, they soon gathered a fashion following. Elitist and style obsessed, they ran with a crowd of like-minded souls who by the end of the 1970s were dressing even more outrageously and starting their own clubs, fashion, and art movements.

Performing as Ziggy Stardust at London's Hammersmith Palais in 1973, David Bowie epitomized glam-rock style. He wore his legendary jockstrap, stockings, platforms, and minidress ensemble. New, super-stylish, and slightly scary, Bowie sent the old rockers packing, and London fashion divided.

Old schoolers like Ossie Clark stuck with Clapton and the Stones, while new bloods like Anthony Price dressed the glam rockers in fitted suits (boys) and corset-boned dresses (girls) in shiny silks and satins.

Glam rock's fun side showed itself in funky T-shirts emblazoned with iconic images like Minnie Mouse, as sold by the boutique Mr. Freedom. At Barbara Hulanicki's Biba store, T-Rex and Roxy Music fans could buy their mainstays of feather boas in pinks, purples, and black; velvet bell-bottoms; and Lurex jackets. Glam rockers also loved the iconic fashion shapes of the 1950s, such as high collars and crepe soles. The 1920s look of dark makeup, fur collars, and slinky retro-style dresses could be found in vintage velvet frock coats, floor-length satin gowns, and diamanté, python, crocodile, and patent-leather accessories. The glam look reached back across the Channel, influencing the work of design houses, including Pierre Balmain and Jean Patou. Fernand Ledoux produced wide-legged, ostrich-trimmed catsuits in 1973, and Ted Lapidus created exquisite jeweled '30s-style evening gowns in

ABOVE AND BELOW FAR LEFT Mr. Freedom Oodles of Poodles satin shirt in western style, early 1970s, with yoke detail. British boutiques such as Mr. Freedom and Granny Takes A Trip sold glam-rock styles to the masses.

BELOW LEFT Mr. Freedom bow-motif yellow satin hotpant playsuit, early 1970s.

OPPOSITE Glitter-rock-influenced jacket and skirt, early 1970s, from British boutique Granny Takes A Trip.

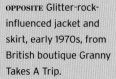

Divine Disco

Disco started out in the clubs of New York and was musically characterized by black dance music, electronically enhanced to provide a souped-up, pounding dance beat or layered orchestral sound. In 1976 Steve Rubell's and Ian Schrager's New York club Studio 54 set the scene. On the dance floor, fabrics sparkled to get you noticed. This was a dance-based look, and nightclubs were packed with women in leotards, footless tights, sparkly leggings, ankle socks with stilettos, silk scarves tied as belts, diamanté hair accessories, and glitter makeup. Fuchsia pink, lilac, and electric blue were favorite colors, while satin, lamé, velour, and other synthetics were the preferred fabrics.

New York designers, including Roy Halston, Bill Blass, and Geoffrey Beene had the grown-up version of the disco look down pat. The form-following, softly draped jersey dresses that Beene had been creating were perfect when translated into sheeny fabrics for the dance floor. Halston made his name as the designer of choice for the Studio 54 A-list crowd. His deep V-necked, backless, Grecian-style silk jersey dresses revealed the perfect parts of his star clients, who included Bianca Jagger and Joan Collins. Sadly, Halston's super-clients deserted when he signed a mass-market diffusion-line contract with J.C. Penney's. Recently regenerated, however, his label is once again becoming synonymous with New York style.

As new silhouettes took over postpunk, designers moved away from snug fitted shapes toward more fluid outlines. By 1978 silk jersey and crepe de chine were being used for new draped shapes, which fell from the neckline or a strapless bodice. Karl Lagerfeld for Chloé created black crepe de chine Grecian-inspired dresses not unlike those of Beene, as well as jackets and skirts that tapered at wrists and ankles. Yves Saint Laurent designed silk pajamas in satin worn with an oversized satin jacket, pulled in at the waist. Sashes, belts, and cummerbunds in gold or colored leather and stiletto sandals in gold or silver completed the look.

In street style the disco look incorporated drainpipe pants in shiny satin, sequined tube tops, and ruched details on skirts and trousers. Shoulders broadened – silk jersey tops featured padded shoulders and front ruching. The British chain Miss Selfridge's black satin slit pencil skirt and matching vest was worn over a sequin tube top, Lurex footless tights, and black stilettos. Details like a pillbox hat with a mini-veil brought the look to life. Other typical outfits included oversized T-shirts sporting roller-disco motifs and tied at the side, and long slinky shirts worn open over a shiny swimsuit and leggings and belted with a scarf. Disco was the last great look of the 1970s, encapsulating the glamorous, thrill-seeking side of fashion's most revolutionary decade.

ABOVE Christian Dior red slit-thigh dress with blouson bodice in silk jersey, mid-1970s.

RIGHT Model standing in front of the towers of Congress, in Brasilia, Brazil, wearing a feather boa and a long gown of opalescent sequins on silk chiffon by Roy Halston, 1973.

Body stockings

A one-piece close-fitting garment made of elastic material and enveloping the whole body like a leotard. Originally worn by dancers, they became popular during the disco craze and was part of the slinky look of fluid 1970s fabrics, which also harked back to 1930s Hollywood glamour.

Maxiskirts

The ankle- or floor-length skirt was a counter to the 1960s miniskirt (considered politically incorrect by many 1970s feminists). In dress form the maxi was often worn with a choker and crocheted shawl and had an A-line skirt with a fitted bodice.

Diana décolleté

An asymmetrical neckline with one bare shoulder, first seen in the second half of the nineteenth century and adopted by Elsa Schiaparelli in the 1930s and Madame Grès in the 1950s, it regained popularity in the late 1970s, especially under the development of Roy Halston.

Wraparound

Diane von Furstenberg's signature wrap dress was a classic that spawned wraparound skirts and tops for the mass market. Her simple knit jersey wrap launched in 1972.

Parkas

A comfortable long outer garment with large pockets, usually made of tough cotton fabric with a removable lining, they were initially designed as an all-weather jacket for soldiers. It became very popular with young people in the 1970s.

Key looks of the decade

1970s

Jumpsuits

One-piece *Charlie's Angels* pantsuit, usually with short legs made of elastic material, such as jersey. Along with this trend came tube dresses, with a reduced figure-hugging outline in solid colors: white, beige, or pastels.

▼Unisex

In the 1970s Rudi Gernreich explored unisex fashion, which he carried to an extreme by using identical clothing on totally hairless male and female models. The androgynous look of Diane Keaton in *Annie Hall*, as below, and musician Patti Smith were part of the trend.

Carmen and gypsy looks

A flamenco style and part of the ethnic fashion of the decade. The look was modeled on the Spanish flamenco costume, usually narrow at the hips, thighs, and knees and ending in a wide skirt, with lace or ruffles at the off-the-shoulder neckline. Similarly, the gypsy look was characterized by frilled or unevenly hemmed skirts worn with blouses tied above the waist.

Gauchos, knickers, and jodhpurs

Mid-length trousers included the calf-length wide-bottomed gauchos, based on South American cowboys; full breeches gathered below the knee; and traditional riding breeches, very full from hip to knee, narrow on the calves, and usually with a leather insert on the inside leg.

▲Caftans

Along with the kimono, the muumuu, the djellaba (a Moroccan hooded robe) or *jalabiya* (a loose Eastern robe), and other styles from India and Africa, caftans became westernized loungewear. They were especially suited to eveningwear when designed in exotic fabrics and edged in metallic trims, as this one in gold thread for Pierre Cardin, 1973.

Folkloric

Every type of ethnic image set a trend. A peasant fashion for eyelets with lacing, braid trim, and false bibbed blouses became universal. The ethnic influence, as seen in this 1970 Zandra Rhodes piece, was so strong that it revived craft skills from far-flung places, seen in Tibetan and Chinese quilted jackets, square-armhole vests, patchwork, and macramé.

Flares and pantsuits

Trousers and pantsuits were serious fashions in the 1970s. They began gently flared, then reached wide bell-bottom proportions by about 1975, after which they slowly reduced to straight and wide until the end of the decade, when they were finally narrow again. Popular fabrics included heavy crepes, wool jersey knits, acrylic jersey, and woven polyester suiting, such as Trevira.

Patterns, prints, and colors

An abundance of floral motifs and nature patterns emerged, although geometrics and stripes continued from the 1960s, albeit in prints and patterns (such as in African and Native American textiles), rather than in form and cut. Typified by a sober neutral palette of white, black, beige, and olive, earth tones were the mark of the day, set off by mustard, brick red, and dark orange.

Eastern influences

Kenzo, Yuki, and Zoran were all 1970s labels that developed from an Eastern minimalist point. As epitomized by Rei Kawakubo and Comme des Garçons, along with Issey Miyake and Yohji Yamomoto, the movement produced clothes that were refined, fluid, and sculptural. In Kawakubo's case, this included ruching and asymmetry.

Hotpants

Coming into fashion in the early 1970s, these were extremely brief shorts that barely covered the bottom and appeared in velvet or Lurex for eveningwear. They were often worn under a buttoned maxi- or midi skirt with the front opened to reveal lots of leg. As is typical of synthetics of the period, these items are rarely found in good condition.

▲Granny dresses

Dresses with empire waistlines, an ornate fabric bodice, and exotic sleeves were popular in a feminine, earth mother way, as was the granny dress, with a high frilled or lace neckline and floral prints on brushed fabric. Laura Ashley contributed to the fashion with her romantic floral cotton prints and deliberately old-fashioned dresses reminiscent of the Victorian era.

Punk

Led by Malcolm McLaren and Vivienne Westwood, the punk movement was deconstructive and anti-Establishment; it was characterized by bondage looks, safety pins, ripped edges, and chaotic irregular stitching. By 1977 Zandra Rhodes was using punk elements, like gold safety pins and chains, to connect and decorate uneven hems and slashed holes edged with gold thread.

▲Disco fashion

Strongly influenced by 1977's *Saturday Night Fever*, disco was characterized by shiny metallic and glittery materials such as sequins, Lurex, and spandex. The pieces, including bandeau tops and stretch skirts, were often adaptations of dancewear that made its way into discos. Gold lamé, leopardskin, and white clothes that glowed in UV lights captured the disco era.

1980s

The 1980s was the decade of "Hard Times" — more than just a song by the Human League and a popular London nightclub, "Hard Times" was a way of life for many. Money, as Mick Hucknall sang, was genuinely "too tight to mention." This was the dawning of the age of Reagan and Thatcher, and the working classes were feeling the pinch. Street fashion, born out of broke fashion students' imaginations and a few ingenious musicians, was adopted as the uniform of the trendy. Those who could afford upscale designer fashion from names like Gianni Versace, Louis Féraud, Claude Montana, and Chanel were wealthy, but not feted for their sense of style. Until clever designers like Jean Paul Gaultier picked up on street accents and adapted them, designer clothing remained a separate entity.

By the middle of the decade, things were looking up. The financial capitals of the world witnessed a boom, and there was a sudden surge of interest in designer shoes, bags, and jewelry — it was the birth of the label. More than ever, New York was a fashion mecca. Calvin Klein, Donna Karan, and Ralph Lauren were the big names, while on another level, hip-hop music began the passion for bling and sportswear tracksuits by Nike, Adidas, and Reebok — teamed with gold chains, medallions, rings, and the latest running shoes — became street fashion's most enduring look.

Nightclubbing was big news on both sides of the Atlantic, and fashion was strongly influenced by the latest club looks. Stephen Sprouse and Norma Kamali dressed New York's clubbers, while individual designers, including Antony Price and John Richmond with Maria Cornejo, made names for themselves on London dance floors. Young single heiresses, including Francesca Thyssen in London and Cornelia Guest in New York, dominated the people pages of style magazines like Andy Warhol's *Interview* in New York and Lord Lichfield's *Ritz* in London.

Tailoring Trends

Tailoring and menswear took off as a major trend, inspired initially by Diane Keaton's _Annie Hall_ character and other unisex looks of the 1970s. Androgynous-looking women, including Annie Lennox of the Eurythmics and model-turned-singer Grace Jones, inspired a new wearable and classic look. Lennox wore a tutu when she sang as a punk with the Tourists but reemerged in a dapper black "mod"-style suit and brogues as a Eurythmic in 1982 – and in so doing quickly became a fashion icon.

Menswear Influences

Early in the decade, pants were left with nowhere to go, having been narrowed into oblivion by punk and installed in the ultimate style ensemble as Yves Saint Laurent's Le Smoking tuxedo. Instead, designers focused on the jacket. Worn on a woman, a male jacket shape made an important and assertive statement. Padded shoulders, pioneered toward the end of the 1970s by Perry Ellis, Thierry Mugler, and Karl Lagerfeld to name a few, made the box-shaped, longer-line jacket the shape of the 1980s.

Giorgio Armani, Gianni Versace, and Calvin Klein took up the slack, creating wearable mannish suit shapes in soft wools, cashmeres, and plaid fabrics in the early part of the decade. A feeling of classic luxury combined with the power of simple tailoring quickly catapulted them to the top of many most-wanted lists.

By 1983, Giorgio Armani had established himself as the number one purveyor of menswear-inspired classical looks. His collections of that year featured lightweight wool suits in monotone shades with blouson jackets and softly draped trousers, along with boxy, square-shaped coats, teamed with simple berets and heels. His designs for the fashion house Erreuno were more grown-up, featuring broad-shouldered monotone tweed coats, shaped in at the waist and tapering to just above the knee.

Armani, Luciano Soprani, Gianfranco Ferré, and Gianni Versace in Milan – and Donna Karan for Anne Klein, Calvin Klein, and Ralph Lauren in New York – created tailored styles tinged with glamour. In 1986, Calvin Klein's summer collection epitomized the new classic with cream flannel trousers, cashmere sweaters, and lightweight wool coats and blazers. Now synonymous with Ralph Lauren, the edged blazer was a strong Klein feature in the early 1980s.

It took a British designer to dilute all this grown-up chic with some humor. For fall/winter 1984, Betty Jackson, who started her own label with husband David Cohen in 1981, reworked Armani-style tailoring into chunkier shapes. Subtle coloring was replaced by bright red, yellow, and blue plaids. Shirts were teamed with matching scarves in purple, yellow, and black boxy prints or dark mustard and red stripes.

1980S MENSWEAR INFLUENCES:

+ Oversized men's-style suit jackets, single- or double-breasted
+ Checks, plaids, and tweeds
+ Belted-in waists and peg-topped gathered trousers
+ Brogues or flat lace-up Dr. Martens shoes
+ Blouson-style jackets in tweed or wool
+ Men's shirts in traditional pale cotton, stripes, or checks
+ Berets or flat caps, suspenders, and cufflinks
+ Ties, either fat and long or skinny

PAGE 182 A Christian Dior dress by Marc Bohan, 1987. Bohan's tenure lasted from 1960 until 1989, and he reworked classic Dior shapes and styles for current times, always in discreet, elegant, and simple designs.

RIGHT Giorgio Armani's mastery of soft tailoring is evident in this menswear-influenced suit, 1984. Early Armani pieces were made in very expensive, luxury fabrics, but his mid-1980s Mani and late 1980s Emporio ranges were developed for a wider market.

OPPOSITE Wool Chanel suits in navy, white, and red, 1983. During the 1980s Lagerfeld revitalized the house of Chanel, producing many variations on the classic tweed suit and introducing the gilt chain belt and other glitzy details.

Unsurprisingly, it was a Frenchman who reworked tailoring once again. Jean Paul Gaultier's 1985 fall/winter menswear collection Wardrobe for Two featured androgyny as a theme, and he went on to design spectacularly feminine-shaped tailoring. Corseted jackets in dark pinstripes with sharp double-breasted fastenings were worn over tapered trousers and pencil skirts. A notable piece was his 1987 dogstooth-check lightweight suit with wide trousers and a long, double-breasted, fitted jacket. Other Gaultier tailored classics included tartan suiting and denim jackets in leopard prints.

The working girl's suit

This was the decade when working women sought to break through the glass ceilings of banking and industry and the image of the modern career woman developed. The film *Working Girl* (1988), starring Melanie Griffith as Sigourney Weaver's beleaguered secretary, echoed the feelings of women working for the female superboss. The uniform was the power suit, a fitted tailored jacket worn over a neat knee-length skirt, an offshoot of the mid-1980s trend for tailoring. Designers were inspired by *Woman's Dress for Success*, John T. Molloy's 1977 book, which suggested that straight skirts, tailored jackets, and feminine takes on the male's office attire was the way forward. Thierry Mugler's form-fitting but stern shapes transmitted the combined air of professional authority and femininity across the boardroom.

New York designers were especially clued-in on the look. By the end of the decade, Richard Tyler and his wife, Lisa Trafficante, had become the city's coolest cutting duo, creating a 1989 womenswear collection of business suits that had the immaculate detailing of London's Savile Row. While New Yorkers worked on masculine styles, Parisians pioneered a more feminine version of the suit. The end of the decade saw suits from Christian Dior in lightweight polka-dot charcoal wool fabrics, with single-breasted jackets and knee-length skirts. Karl Lagerfeld reworked the classic Chanel bouclé suit with brass buttons in navy and cream, and it quickly became the media and fashion boss's favorite. In Britain, Roland Klein and Bruce Oldfield made feminine versions of the power suit in lighter wool fabrics, dropping waists on jackets for a blouson effect, as with Klein, or softly gathering skirts for a feminine effect, as with Oldfield.

ABOVE LEFT Red 1980s dress with one-shoulder neckline and oblong keyhole opening, by German designer Thierry Mugler. Mugler worked in a variety of different materials, from taffeta, lace, and raffia to chrome, latex, and plastic.

ABOVE AND RIGHT Lime Thierry Mugler suit, 1980s. The designer's overtly sexy, fetishistic silhouette was defined by broad shoulders and a defined waist, making his extreme proportions almost body distortions. His body-fitted designs were controlled and highly structured.

OPPOSITE A 1989 automotive-inspired dress by Thierry Mugler. Mugler took delight in industrial styling, which he displayed in his geometries of detailing and his references to such themes as 1950s cars.

Body-conscious Fashion

Body-conscious styling crept into fashion in the mid-1980s, when most women had exhausted the androgynous and clumsy oversized looks of the beginning of the decade. Wool, jersey, cotton drill, velvet, and denim all appeared on the market in stretch versions, and designers had no trouble styling sexy formfitting garments in the new fabrics. By the end of the decade, Jean Paul Gaultier was dressing models in fitted corsets with pointed conical breasts, sparking the trend for underwear as outerwear.

Thanks largely to the development of Lycra and its use as an outerwear fabric and not just for lingerie and swimwear, many new fashion shapes were born. Azzedine Alaïa, sold through Joseph Ettedgui's stores in London, created dresses in thick cream, chocolate brown, and black stretchy fabrics for spring/summer 1987, which sold out in days. He arrived on the fashion scene via side-laced, sexy creations in 1985 and went on to produce formfitting fashion's most iconic looks. In 1987 he teamed sleeveless tank-style and long-sleeved, scoop-necked dresses with matching opaque pantyhose and shoes, creating a streamlined overall look fashionistas loved. Opaque pantyhose has stayed in style, though it remains considerably easier to lay one's hands on than an Alaïa original. A famous look from 1988 featured models in black Lycra minidresses with white shirting details, waist-cinching black leather belts, slicked back hair, and red lips.

Jean Paul Gaultier's 1983 Dadaiste collection heralded the arrival of the corset dress. Fitted in satin or thick stretchy Lycra with built-in corset top and lacing, the dress sparked a million copies. The Russian

ABOVE Grace Jones and Azzedine Alaïa, 1985. Grace wears a corset-strapped dress in Lycra stretch. Called the King of Cling, Alaïa mastered the spiral and crisscross seaming that lengthens the leg and lifts the bosom and bottom, while the stretch fabric clings to the curves of the body. His designs are often constructed from many smaller interlinking pieces.

RIGHT Bodymap's The Cat In The Hat Takes A Rumble With The Techno Fish collection, in 1984, shows dresses with graphic patterns by Hilde Smith. The concept of Bodymap was to restructure fabric around the body, creating areas that reveal and conceal the body. The designers were clearly influenced both by Japanese avant-garde and by Vivienne Westwood.

Biker collection of 1986 combined fitted garments with fun styling. A striped dress was reminiscent of a road cyclist's ensemble. It was sexy and fun dressing, and the long fitted stretchy skirt became a signature Gaultier piece. The Rock Star collection of 1987 showcased Gaultier's love of such iconic pieces as the denim jacket, reworked into fitted leopard-print or black leather. Most famously, his rock-star looks led him to a meeting with Madonna; the rest, as they say, is history.

Sportswear and dancewear influences

In New York, sporty, stretchy, and jersey fabrics were pioneered in the designs of Perry Ellis during the late 1970s. Hot on the heels of disco, body-hugging fabrics became cool, not just for dancing and partying. In 1980, New Yorker Norma Kamali produced a collection fashioned entirely from sporty fleece-type fabric. In gray sweatshirting, a utilitarian fabric used for years in American active sportswear, Kamali produced drop-waisted full skirts, dresses, jumpsuits, long raglan-sleeved jackets and tops, rollneck dresses, and leggings. Offering style with comfort, it soon launched a new trend.

Such looks also drew upon stretchy fun fashion pieces designed by the groundbreaking duo Bodymap in 1981. David Holah and Stevie Stewart were London fashion graduates who enjoyed brief fame with their immensely fun and wearable fishtail skirts, cropped trousers, short jackets, and long or large-looped knits. Other London designers, including Helen Robinson's PX label, developed the trend, producing wraparound jersey skirts, turbans, and tops, which became a fashion staple during the first half of the decade.

ABOVE AND LEFT Bodymap cardigan and skirt with textile detail, mid-1980s. Designed to shape the body, the pieces had holes in unexpected places, as on the sleeves and shoulders here. Designers David Holah and Stevie Stewart used multiple layered prints in their textile designs.

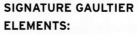

**SIGNATURE GAULTIER
ELEMENTS:**

- Fitted shapes
- Seams on the outside
- Corset styling, lace-up basque-style torsos
- Shaped bra tops on dresses
- Bra tops worn with rolled up men's jeans
- Biker-style leather jackets
- Stretch turtlenecks in black or primary-colored stripes
- Black houndstooth plaid suiting
- Sailor navy-and-white stripes

LEFT Jean-Paul Gaultier corset, 1987, worn on top of a cream-colored sweater and miniskirt with white leggings. His corsetry and bondage influences can be seen in his use of fetishistic fabric like rubber and vinyl, as seen in the white corset he made for Madonna's 1990 Blond Ambition tour.

ABOVE AND RIGHT The late 1980s Jean Paul Gaultier corset dress defined the "inner wear as outer wear" moment in fashion history.

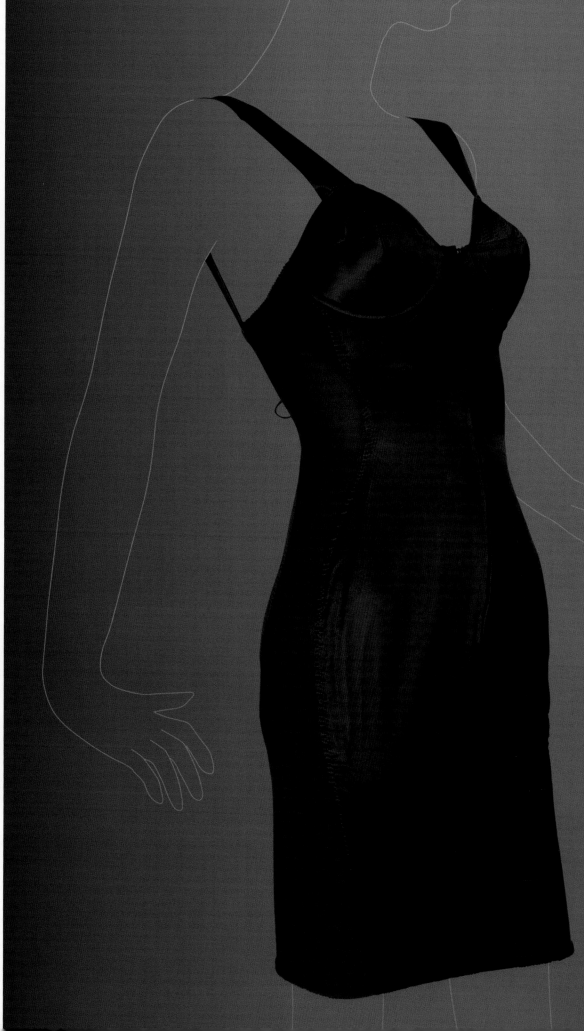

Bustles in Hedgerows

Skirt shapes went wild in the 1980s. After decades of A-lines and soft drapes, it was time for a change. Enter the puffball, ra-ra, and mini-crini, the look that put Vivienne Westwood firmly on the international fashion map. As the 1970s faded out, skirt shapes became pretty tired. Softly draped tulip shapes and pencil skirts were sold in stores nationwide, while designers dabbled with fluid shapes, following in the footsteps of successful New Yorkers like Roy Halston and Geoffrey Beene. Then in spring 1983, the masterful Yves Saint Laurent shook everything up with new neat, feminine shapes featuring nipped-in waists, fuller skirts, and shorter jackets. As so often happens in fashion, other international design houses produced similar looks, including Calvin Klein in New York, Missoni with full skirts in Milan, and Chantal Thomas in Paris. Thomas's delightful collection featured cinched waists, puffed sleeves, and grown-up buttoned-up jumpers.

Vivienne Westwood created a series of wacky collections following the largely London-based success of her Pirates/Buccaneer and Buffalo collections in 1981 and 1982, respectively. Featuring layered shapes – and underwear as outerwear in the case of the Buffalo Gals, who wore bras over the top of wooly sweaters and full, hitched-up skirts – there was some semblance of female shaping. But it was to take the introduction of Westwood's mini-crinoline in 1985 to really cement the full skirt shape and send fashion off in a brand-new direction. The mini-crini was a short, hooped skirt based on Victorian outlines, worn with over-the-knee cotton stockings and flat or clumpy shoes. Teamed with short fitted blazers in lightweight wool patterns and stripes, the look was seized upon by chain-store retailers. However, the quality and cutting of the fabric was difficult to copy, so lots of cheaper versions hit the streets with appalling results!

After the mini-crini came the puffball, designed by Christian Lacroix in 1986 for his 1987 spring/summer collection, which earned him the Golden Thimble prize, couture's highest award. The crini and puffball were swiftly followed by the ra-ra, a two- or three-tiered short skirt, which became standard dress for the average girl in 1986 and 1987. Tutus also reemerged in collections by Lacroix, Moschino, and Chanel, toward the end of the decade.

ABOVE A model displays a styled Spanish ensemble, black jacket embroidered over a balloon dress and Castilian hat for Christian Lacroix, 1987. His puffball (pouf) skirt was a thigh-high version of this dress.

ABOVE In 1985 Vivienne Westwood launched her mini-crini – a short hooped skirt inspired by the Victorian crinoline and made in tweed or cotton. The shape brought back an hourglass silhouette in place of the inverted triangle so popularized by the power suit trend.

RIGHT A polka-dot mid-1980s mini-crini by Vivienne Westwood. The mini-crini designs incorporated prints in harlequins, stripes, and dots, which were cartoonish and childlike in feel; the one here directly references Minnie Mouse. Westwood would continue to look to historical costume for years to come.

On the Street

Streetwear took on new dimensions as designers operating entirely separately from couture and high fashion created arty super-trendy looks fueled by politics and passion. In London, street fashion was inspired by clubs and nightlife. In New York, it had roots in a number of different movements, from hip-hop and world music to punk rock and pop art. Jean-Charles de Castelbajac was a Parisian who loved the work of New York artists such as Andy Warhol, Robert Indiana, and Keith Haring, and he incorporated Haring's graphic human prints into garments toward the end of the decade. Haring had been a graffiti artist, but his trademark prints also appeared on jackets by Vivienne Westwood in her 1983 collection.

Other trendsetting New Yorkers included Norma Kamali, whose sporty, stretch clothes were inspired by the street sportswear of hip-hop fans. Their brightly colored professional sportswear had yet to filter into mainstream fashion, but the stretch and stripes of Adidas, Nike, and Reebok worn on the street proved inspirational for Kamali. Away from the catwalks, a punkier attitude pervaded New York. Stephen Sprouse had begun his career assisting Roy Halston in the 1970s but broke away to design pop fashion classics. Finally setting up his own label in 1984, he went on to dress such icons as Debbie Harry in his signature brightly colored 1960s-style leatherette minidresses.

Graphic word-prints made dramatic statements on the catwalk for Katharine Hamnett in her fall/winter 1984 collection. Politics were the issue, with "Worldwide Nuclear Ban Now" a key slogan, and Hamnett's oversized T-shirts became the trendy choice for young Londoners. Hamnett herself famously attended a fashion reception with Prime Minister Margaret Thatcher, wearing a T-shirt bearing the slogan "58% Don't Want Pershing" (American missiles). The image and message were taken on board by rock band Frankie Goes To Hollywood, with their 1984 hit song "Relax"; part of their gimmick was to wear oversized Hamnett T-shirts bearing the word "Relax," an enduring image of the decade.

Street fashion was just that, so it was hard to buy the look off the rack. Successful British designers who moved from designing street looks to selling single pieces and even, occasionally, whole collections to boutiques included Bodymap, Wendy Dagworthy, Rachel Auburn, and Dexter Wong, to name a few. Wong dressed Boy George and sold his funky big jackets, long dress coats, and tartan trousers. Other street trends included rockabilly, ragamuffin, and goth, but the looks were created by kids in their bedrooms or rock band stylists and were never really available in fashion boutiques.

ABOVE AND ABOVE LEFT A bold graffiti-inspired jacket with inside label detail from Jean-Charles de Castelbajac, mid-1980s. Using strong colors and workaday materials in haute couture, he is called a humanist designer with a propensity for fun and eccentricity. He collaborated with artists in producing his "picture garments," inscribed with a different artist's work every season.

ABOVE Front and back views of a Vivienne Westwood bomber jacket from the Witches collection, 1983, decorated with a work by New York graffiti artist Keith Haring. The collection marked the end of the Westwood and McLaren partnership.

Colors and Prints

The 1980s was the decade when color came back into fashion. Bright primaries and bold monotones, vivid prints, dots, and stripes dominated. This was no time for shrinking violets. Designers went fabric mad. Many collections were led by the fabric, the styling following as a sort of afterthought. Nobody looked particularly great in giant polkadots or deckchair stripes, but that didn't stop Claude Montana, the Emanuels, and a host of others from putting them on the scene.

Bold colors

As the decade dawned, fuchsia pink had made its way to the forefront of fashion. After the muted purples, browns, and beiges of the 1970s, this was a welcome arrival. The Italian fashion houses of Milan loved color, particularly Gianni Versace and knitwear guru Missoni. Versace cofounded the label with his brother Santo in 1978; flamboyant, luxurious color was a staple from the start, and the Versace house style evolved to become the most glamorous label in the world by 1990. In 1982, royal blue, red, and gold swirls decorated a sexy bodice, while blue and black chiffon stripes with a peek of red beneath made up a slashed up-the-front skirt.

Gianfranco Ferré, meanwhile, produced black-topped dresses with skirts that resembled huge satin sashes in intense blues, reds, and yellows in 1982. Intense colors became key elements for many designers. Claude Montana mixed them with navy for a nautically themed collection in 1983. In New York, Norma Kamali sent models out in vivid yellow plastic skirt suits with oversized blazers. Less traditional shapes, but even brighter colors came through from Thierry Mugler; his 1984 collection featured lime-green stretch velour dresses with raglan sleeves, his trademark skullcaps in white, and oversized canvas raincoats in a combination of bright colors.

Neutrals and simplicity

A welcome antidote to bright colors and overtly feminine styling came from Japanese designers, notably Issey Miyake, Rei Kawakubo of Commes des Garçons, and Yohji Yamamoto. Favoring monotones or neutrals, Yamamoto brought the black turtleneck back into fashion in 1986, teaming it with black hoisery, Dr. Martens boots, and simple wool coats. In 1982 Kawakubo's black "lace" wool sweater, oversized and full of holes, followed on from the "rags" of her 1981 neutral, exposed-seamed separates. By 1987, Commes des Garçons had changed direction slightly, producing more formal, black tailoring of oversized jumpers, jackets, and trousers worn with crisp white shirts. Issey Miyake, meanwhile, focused on pleated silks in neutral colors, wrapped around the body into tube shapes. In 1985 he produced the famous bamboo bodice, part of his Body Works: Fashion Without Taboos exhibition at London's Victoria & Albert Museum.

LEFT Nautical offerings from Claude Montana, 1983, best known for his leather work and extreme broad shoulders. The striped top, jacket, and pantaloons give a New Romantics shape.

OPPOSITE Karl Lagerfeld's graphic print knitwear, 1984, shows the bold gestures and black-and-white themes that defined textiles in the 1980s.

Fabrics and Textiles

Never before in fashion history had so many fabrics competed for center stage. Postpunk, leather and tartan were adapted into mainstream looks, and many designers attempted to move denim upscale. The "stretch" movement, brought about by the developments in Lycra and dancewear fads, had a huge impact, as did sportswear jersey (see pages 188–9), but the textures of denim, leather, parachute silk, and tweed were also liberally apparent.

Denim and jean fashions

Although denim was fashioned into every kind of garment during the 1980s, jeans remained a fashion stalwart. At the start of the decade, designer jeans by Calvin Klein had just been introduced. Gaultier took denim design a step further, stretching the denim jacket into a tailored, hourglass shape in 1986. Made of dark-colored denim with otherwise traditional fastenings, it sold out in stores almost immediately. Yet this remains one of the few designer denim success stories of the decade. The mid-market company Guess made a huge noise with its 1987 campaign featuring a Bardot-esque Claudia Schiffer in a basque, gold hoop earrings, and Guess jeans, but on the whole, denim stayed downscale.

Leather styling

Claude Montana and Thierry Mugler had the most impact on leather as a fashion fabric. Mugler had honed his skills in the 1970s, creating bronzed leather space-age catsuits with matching skullcaps. Montana is credited with turning women on to high-fashion leather. Blouson jackets, fitted leather pants, and plain miniskirts in lambskin dyed purple, black, fuchsia, or royal blue were his most-wanted items. Throughout the 1980s, Montana's design silhouette of huge shoulders and nipped-in waist became synonymous with his name. In 1983, military detailing added a new dimension, and suits with long-line skirts and jackets in beige or black were decorated with epaulettes, studded belts, and metal details. A black-and-red swimsuit line featured matching black leather jackets with red leather turnback cuffs and detailing. Some of Montana's most wearable designs emerged in 1987 and 1988, such as knee-length black stretch dresses featuring leather inserts that fitted in at the waist around sexy front zippers, and miniskirts and zip-up jackets with leather detailing. In Italy, Versace produced cropped, oversized black leather biker jackets for fall 1984, which are highly wearable today.

Textures

Parachute silk was one of the decade's most-used and prettiest fabrics, featuring in Katharine Hamnett's 1984 collection in vivid red, green, and yellow, cut into simple tops, parachute pants, or oversized sleeveless dresses with matching duster coats. Tartan appeared in Vivienne Westwood's and Betty Jackson's tailoring, "growing up" from punk influences into a favored suiting fabric.

OPPOSITE Designer Geoffrey Beene's gray satin, drop-waist ensembles with black floral patterns and stripes, 1984. The unconventional Beene frequently used black-and-white neutrals and fluid modernist forms.

BELOW Another example of mixing fabrics, textures, and patterns in one garment is this leather-and-jersey dress by British designer Anna Bank, mid-1980s.

OPPOSITE Light-blue 1980s leather jacket, by American designer Allison Goulard. Note the built-up, conical spirals in the sleeve, classic 1980s oversized rounded shoulders, tapered cuffs, and asymmetrical hem. The jacket is likely to have been worn with high-waisted black ski pants or matching straight-cut leather mini.

ABOVE Jean-Paul Gaultier 1980s animal-print jacket. His clothes have a kind of kitschy glamour that made them popular show-off items. He used details such as metal tips on collars, and his jackets were highly structured and fitted to exaggerate the female body.

Evening Glitz

The 1980s evening gown is a classic that works for two reasons: First, the sleek feminine lines accentuate all a woman's curves, no matter what her size or shape, and second, the fabrics are also female-friendly – no woman can fail to look good in a matte-black crepe de chine. Dresses from the era were varied, the best versions having draped or cowl necks, or slashed or boat necklines. Batwing sleeves were stunning, as were full long sleeves with cuffs. Other features were deep V-necks, high turtleneck collars, and cutaway backs.

Eveningwear master Antony Price began as a menswear designer, creating looks for Bryan Ferry in the 1970s. At the 1985 Fashion Aid, a huge event staged at the Albert Hall in London by Bob Geldof, Price dressed his muse Jerry Hall in a peplum-waist creation in red, orange, and gold sparkling brocade that stole the show. This was not typical Price, who was famous for boned, fitted bodices, simple lines, and sexy satin fabrics. Besides the famous "mermaid" fish-tailed evening dress, he is credited with bringing men's tailoring to women's eveningwear. His dresses were named "resultwear" because they always got the right results!

Christian Lacroix created the decade's newest evening outlines in 1986, with fitted bodices and short puffball skirts. For years, women had stuck to classic floor-length ballgowns, but the black-tie event "came out" as a fashion parade ground in the 1980s. Heady with the success of the cocktail and eveningwear explosion, which came hand in hand with the mini-economic boom, the Parisian designers went over the top, design-wise. Jean-Louis Scherrer created the ruched satin mini evening dress in 1987. With huge ruffles around strapless tops, drop-waist, tutu-style skirts, back bustles, bows, and ribbons, these pastel-colored, short dresses were copied everywhere. In 1987 Yves Saint Laurent and Emanuel Ungaro took evening dresses even shorter. Ungaro's version featured ruched satin skirts in plain chocolate brown, teamed with pink details that included rose corsages and ankle-trailing sashes. Saint Laurent produced cream ostrich-feather confections.

Some American and Italian designers had a different approach to eveningwear. Luxurious satins and velvets came in black, brown, or beige. Donna Karan's black Lycra "body" of 1984 was worn with a simple wraparound full skirt as an antidote to the "hysteria" in Europe. Giorgio Armani produced floor-length, sequined sheaths in neutral colors. Other designers, including Michael Klein, experimented with much simpler graphic designs – a 1989 piece in black viscose features a slash, knee-length supersimple sheath, built onto a conical bra shape.

OPPOSITE Antony Price black velvet evening dress, mid-1980s. Price's evening gowns had intricate corsetry and interfacing to achieve the remarkable shapes, which created an old-style Hollywood glamour that reverberated with his rock-star clients. Here his magnificent show-stopping dress is all about over-the-top 1980s excess.

RIGHT As Henry Ford once allegedly said of his automobiles, you can have "any color so long as it's black," and this can be said of evening dresses in the 1980s, when black was first pick for the fashion pack. Here a tulle train and broken sequin decoration adds brilliance to a 1980s Chanel evening gown designed by Karl Lagerfeld. Already successful as the name behind fashion house Chloé, Lagerfeld became artistic director of Chanel in 1983, adding his own dynamic twists to traditional Chanel shapes and fabrics.

The Avant-Garde

If back to nature was the fashion theme of the 1970s, into the future was the mood when 1980 dawned. Oddities, quirky shapes, bisexual looks, and sculpted fabrics provided the materials for the new avant-garde. Many artists turned to fashion as a vehicle for expression; many fashion designers, in turn, were inspired by art. New fabrics, cutting techniques, and manufacturing methods made it easier to create flimsy, cutout fabrics, as in Rei Kawakubo for Comme des Garçons' knitwear or Issey Miyake's laminated polyester breastplate from his 1982 collection. Miyake's 1980s designs are dramatic: multistitched, layered cloaks with deep hoods and space-age pink satin minidresses with stand-away yoke collars, worn with chiffon fingerless gloves and stockings, were two of his more wearable 1983 masterpieces.

The avant-garde in fashion existed on two levels. On the street, New Romantics spent the beginning of the decade heading out for the evening dressed in perhaps a black shroud with a totally shaved white-powdered head with one purple eyebrow. Extreme dressing was a mode of self-expression. Naturally, extreme looks suited very few, so the real collector's pieces were created by either Japanese or a few young Western designers who recognized a woman's need to wear as well as display clothes.

With his first collection, 1983's "Les Incroyables," John Galliano, fresh out of London's St. Martin's College of Art and Design, introduced a new word to fashion: *deconstructionist*. The process of producing garments that look almost finished or fit the wearer in new or unconventional ways marked his collection and became a movement in the 1980s. Inspired by the clothes of the French Revolution, Galliano's frock coats with exposed seams, upside-down-looking skirts, and stiff organdy shirts decorated with broken-up chandelier necklaces were an immediate success.

Galliano's collection heralded the return from Victorian times of the frock coat, a garment much beloved by deconstructionist designers, including Yohji Yamamoto, whose black 1987 version featured a red tulle bustle. Yamamoto's early 1981 collection was called "oblique chic" by *Vogue*, referring to his misshapen asymmetrical lines. He worked draping and wrapping around the body and took the ideas for the shaping from the fabric itself.

Yamamoto and Kawakubo paved the way for a new wave of deconstructionist designers. Martin Margiela, a young Belgian, made his debut in 1989 with appealing tailored separates, which seemed to fasten incorrectly, or simply be the wrong size — yet once on, fitted perfectly. After the powered-up leather, mixed colors, and aggressively feminine shaping of tailoring, deconstructionism provided a welcome alternative.

FAR RIGHT Lace knitwear
by Rei Kawakubo for
Comme des Garçons, 1982.
Her deconstructed sweaters,
incorporating rips, holes,
and tears that recall
intricate webs, were labeled
post-atomic by the press.
Kawakubo was known for
her complex cut, random
ruching, asymmetrical
seams and hems, crinkled
surfaces, and unfinished
edges. This piece seems to
recall Vivienne Westwood's
Hangman's pulloverr
(see page 172).

RIGHT A fluidly asymmetrical
1980s dress by John
Galliano, showing his
inventive cutting and
draping skills. The
complicated cut and
asymmetrical draping
are fully revealed only
when on the wearer.

OPPOSITE A 1980s Comme
des Garçons dress that
exhibits the distinctive
masterly cutting, knotting,
and draping techniques of
Rei Kawakubo.

Androgyny
Style setters who included
Annie Lennox and Grace Jones
made the androgynous look big
news with men's suits, ties, and
close-cropped hair, combined
with the ultimate feminine
touch – red lips or a corset-
style basque.

▶Streetwear
Letters, numbers, and graphics
made the oversized T-shirt the
most popular single item in
the 1980s. New York artist Keith
Haring, his work shown here in
a design for Vivienne Westwood,
created simple graphic drawings
that popped up everywhere.

Full skirts and layering
Vivienne Westwood's
multilayered full skirts
and sweaters worn
with bras over the
top and chunky boots
epitomized the street-
urchin look.

White prairie skirts
Pioneers and prairie girls at
Ralph Lauren and English roses
at Laura Ashley wore white
lace and eyelet-lace skirts and
dresses. Full tiered skirts with
peasant tops, accessorized with
brown leather belts and purses,
finished the look.

Key looks
of the decade

1980s

▲Stripes and tartan
Color was riotous – Betty
Jackson and Wendy Dagworthy
sent models down runways
in bulky multicolored tweeds.
Short kilts and other traditional
clothing returned, albeit in
subverted styling.

Wide cinch belts
The cinched-in waist was
the keypoint of 1980s dressing.
A curvaceous silhouette came
back into style, with belts making
a huge impact.

▶Suits and shoulders

The television program *Dynasty* helped the power suit catch on worldwide, but couture had led the way: black-and-white houndstooth pencil skirts with a nipped-in jacket by Marc Bohan for Christian Dior and Giorgio Armani's "Donna" ad campaign 1984 to '85 were notable. Here, a black-and-white 1983 Jean-Louis Scherrer suit exhibits the extreme styling of the silhouette.

Oversized

Oversized looks featured in many catwalk collections, from Katharine Hamnett to Issey Miyake to Kenzo. This oversized shirtdress, based on a man's work shirt, but with deep side slits, is worn with an oversized black leather belt.

Puffball skirts

Christian Lacroix brought this little gem into style in 1986, hot on the heels of Vivienne Westwood's mini-crini.

Asymmetrics

Slashed shoulders and halfway hems, one-sleeve wonders, and black Lycra with cutouts were prevalent. Couture versions included Comme des Garçons designs, especially as they appeared on Kim Basinger in the film *9 1/2 Weeks* (1986).

◀Laura Ashley dresses

Reaching her apogee in the early 1980s, Laura Ashley brought a sweet femininity to women's dresses that worked as a counter to the power suit, as shown at left. The clothes had a neo-Victorian, Old World romanticism that seemed to find relevance in the conservative ethos of the time.

Shopping Guide *by Mark and Cleo Butterfield*

Most people who collect and wear designer fashions do so simply because of the sheer pleasure involved. The hunt for a good piece, the knowledge you gain in the process, and the personal stories you hear along the way can be as compelling as finding and purchasing a highly desired, sought-after piece. Whether your aim is collecting a specific designer or within a particular time period, or finding a unique piece you know no one else will have or wear, there are a few ground rules and tips to keep in mind that will help you locate the best pieces for you.

First of all, know what you are buying. There really is no substitute for the experience gained from seeing and handling vintage pieces.

Where to buy
Specialist vintage fashion fairs and markets are a great opportunity to meet a lot of dealers and see a huge variety of classic vintage clothing gathered together in one place. Specialist shops and viewings at major auction houses are also excellent places to see a high concentration of quality pieces. Here you can familiarize yourself with clothes from different periods and the work of specific designers.

Online auctions such as eBay can be full of pitfalls for the unwary. First, the seller is unlikely to be a vintage dealer and may know very little about the garment her or she is auctioning. Without there having been any deliberate attempt to mislead, items are quite frequently incorrectly assigned to periods or accredited to designers. Second, there's no way of seeing the item to check its condition. Always email the seller about stains, repairs, alterations, etc., and ask to see the label if it hasn't been shown.

Buying tips
❖ Never buy a stained garment with the hope that it will come out with washing or dry cleaning. If the mark's been there for a long time, it probably isn't going to shift. Get a full description of stains, such as rust, mildew, or sweat, as well as any odors.

❖ Always check the item thoroughly for condition. Hold it up to the light to reveal any moth holes. Check both sides of the fabric for scorches, tears, mended areas, missing beadwork or embellishments, and for disintegration of any type. Any professional seller will automatically point out tears or other signs of damage, but always ask.

❖ Focus on a particular time period or designer; you will gain deeper knowledge about a specialized subject and meet like-minded buyers and sellers who will further your experience and be able to give you

"Fashion is not something that exists in dresses only... fashion has to do with ideas, the way we live, what is happening."
Coco Chanel

more information on the subject. This will also help you focus on your aim, rather than trying to pick from what you like of a century's worth of designs.

❖ If you are buying for a collection or investment, look for pieces that typify a designer's work, and always buy the best pieces that you can afford.

❖ If you are buying to wear the clothes, follow the sizing tips on page 210, so that you choose the era that best suits your body shape and inherent style; otherwise, you may feel uncomfortable or as if you are wearing a costume, rather than a piece that makes you look and feel great.

❖ Couture dresses claim the highest prices, but the price also depends on the designer, age, workmanship, condition, and size; if you are focused on a specific designer, for example, you may compromise on size or condition to own it. Alternatively, you may accept an unauthenticated piece if the detailing is remarkably rare or beautiful.

❖ Many sellers use standard descriptions to indicate the condition of the garment: **mint** is rare and perfect, probably never worn; **near mint** indicates light wear, as in evening dresses; **excellent** means it is sound with some wear but no flaws; **very good** indicates minor flaws or stains but otherwise high quality; **good** means that it is wearable but shows some deterioration.

Dating garments

Once you have some experience handling period garments, you will develop an intrinsic sense of the time period. A knowledge of the fabrics, notions, and stitching techniques typical of the time will also give you good indications of the era. Familiarize yourself with fabric and trimming terms from past eras, and learn the difference between them and when they were in common use. The glossary on pages 217-19 will help, as will the further reading on page 223. Construction methods and the silhouette of the garment are also good indicators – for example, garments were much more fitted before 1960. The underlying structure of the piece will also offer clues as to whether the piece is couture or ready-to-wear, in the case of missing labels, and the value and age of the piece.

If the designer or label is known, this may help you identify the date by the time period the designer was active. Many designers changed the style of their name or label over time, or were affiliated with various brands – see pages 214-16 for the glossary, which lists the labels designers worked under.

When attempting to date garments, here are a few additional guidelines to help you pinpoint the date.

❖ Garment care labels came into popular use only after 1971.

"*The truly fashionable are beyond fashion.*"
Cecil Beaton

- Zippers were in use in the 1920s for heavy-duty fastenings, boots, and so on, but are not common in dresses until the 1930s.
- Plastic zippers were introduced in the 1930s, but constructed along the same lines as metal zippers, with individual teeth. Nylon coil zippers came into common use in the 1960s.
- Zippers usually appeared in side seams up until the 1950s, and later appeared in the center back of dresses and skirts and the center front of trousers.
- Most British prewar clothes were dressmaker-made and won't have labels.
- Machine overlocking of seams, done by the serger machine, came into use in the United States in the 1920s.

Sizes

Many pre-Second World War garments – especially in Britain and on the Continent – were dressmaker-made and thus will have no size labels, as they were made for a specific person's shape. In the United States too many women made (and still make) their own clothes. So for such a dress to fit you perfectly, you also have to be that same size. Standardization of sizes only came in with mass production. A 1960s or 1970s size would be expected to be two or more sizes smaller than a modern one, but waist measurements were proportionately smaller, so make sure you can try it on, or get all the measurements.

Thanks to better nutrition and exercise habits, however, women today are taller and bigger than ever before, so there's no substitute for trying the item on. If this isn't possible, ask for the seller to provide exact measurements, including not only length, waist, and bust measurements but also the hip, cuff, sleeve length, neck opening, from nape to waist, back shoulder to shoulder, waist to hem, shoulder to hem, the circumference of the hemline, and any potentially restrictive areas, like under the upper arm.

In general, 1920s fashions generally suit the small and slight of figure; 1950s clothes are created along the hourglass line, so they fit the curvaceous, though waists are very small; 1960s fashions are best on the tall and leggy.

Couture items

Many couture pieces are works of art, highly hand-constructed or hand-embellished and made of the finest materials available at the time. Authenticating a couture item can be very difficult; often, the lining of a garment would wear through and be cut away, and along with it the label. Additionally, the best pieces are those made to measure, as a great deal of labor and craftsmanship went into the pieces; the name of the individual client often appears on the dress label.

Because these items will never be created again, and the level of artistry involved can never be repeated due to cost and expertise limitations, couture items are highly covetable. Pieces showing exquisite handworked beading or embroidery, unique hand-dyed colors, luxury fabrics, or unique techniques, such as Fortuny pleating, are especially desirable. Keep these, and the tips below, in mind when looking for couture:

❖ Labels with the designer's name, an ink number, and the client's name
❖ Stitching that is fine, neat, and even
❖ A garment in good condition is likely to have been well cared for
❖ Careful sewing of buttons, buttonholes, hooks, and other closures, and fabric-covered or concealed fasteners
❖ Lining and interior structure that is as well crafted as the exterior

Care and storage
If you are ever in doubt about whether a piece should be washed, consult a professional conservator or ask a costume dealer for advice, especially if you suspect the piece may be rare or if you are unsure of the fragility of its materials. Do not ever use a washing machine or dryer for vintage pieces, and think carefully about pressing any item, as it can press stains into the fabric. Steaming is usually a good option for robust fabrics.

There is a risk that moths, carpet beetles, or their eggs could be lurking in the fibers of your latest vintage purchase, and they will happily destroy the rest of your wardrobe. Wrap the piece in acid-free tissue paper, place it in a sealed plastic bag, and put it in the freezer for three days. Be gentle when removing it, especially if it is silk, and allow it to gradually to defrost. Here are a few general tips you can follow:

❖ Always clean any new item before storing. If the garment has a cleaning label that says it can be washed, it is always safer to hand wash. If there is no label and you think that it ought to be washable (for example, if it's made of cotton), test an inconspicuous part first.
❖ Modern detergent powders may be too harsh and cause colours to run, so use a pure soap powder such as Lux.
❖ Never wash a 1920s sequin dress, as the sequins are made of gelatin, and will dissolve in the water!
❖ Many older fabrics are not color-fast and may discolor, shrink, or distort, particularly any that are based on silk, acetate, or rayon.
❖ Consider not only the fabric of the piece, but also any trims or linings.
❖ Dry cleaning is damaging to many fabrics, and may require the removal of labels or accessories, which will devalue the piece.
❖ Don't store anything in plastic. Natural fibers will hold moisture, and once housed in the mini-greenhouse of a plastic cover will release the water that may mark your garment. Wrap it in acid-free tissue and keep it in a cardboard box.

Collections & Stores

Museums & Collections

UNITED KINGDOM

Design Museum
Shad Thames
London SE1 2YD
Tel: (+44) 870-833-9955
Email: info@designmuseum.org
Website: www.designmuseum.org
A showcase for all design genres,
including fashion.

The Fashion and Textile Museum
88 Bermondsey Street
London SE1 3XF
Tel: (+44) 207-407-8664
Email: info@ftmlondon.org
Website: www.ftmlondon.org
Opened by Zandra Rhodes. Shows the
best of vintage and modern fashion
and textiles, with rotating exhibitions
featuring such designers as Vivienne
Westwood and Ossie Clark.

Gallery of Costume
Platt Hall, Rusholme
Manchester M14 5LL
Tel: (+44) 161-224-5217
www.manchestergalleries.org
One of Britain's largest collections of clothing
and accessories, dating from the seventeenth
century to the present day.

Museum of Costume
Bennett Street
Bath BA1 2QH
Tel: (+44) 1225-477-173
Email: costume_enquiries@bathnes.gov.uk
Website: www.museumofcostume.co.uk
Eveningwear from the 1900s to the 1950s,
as well as iconic 1960s and 1970s designs.
Annual exhibitions highlighting
a particular aspect of fashion.

Victoria and Albert Museum
Cromwell Road
London SW7 2RL
Tel: (+44) 207-942-2000
Email: textilesandfashion@vam.ac.uk
Website: www.vam.ac.uk
Fashion and textile collection dating
from the seventeenth century to the
present day, with an emphasis on
influential European design. Also
showcases accessories such as gloves,
jewelry, and handbags.

UNITED STATES

Chicago History Museum
Clark Street at North Avenue
Chicago, IL 60614-6071
Tel: 312-642-4600
Website: www.chicagohs.org
A collection of 50,000 pieces, including
historical costumes and designer items by
such names as Charles Worth, Paul Poiret,
and Issey Miyake.

Cornell Costume and Textile Collection
Department of Textiles and Apparel
Cornell University
Ithaca, NY 14853-4401
Tel: 607-255-2235
Email: caj7@cornell.edu
Website (curator): www.human.cornell.edu
Website (online gallery):
costume.cornell.edu/greetingdb.htm
A collection of more than 9,000 items, a
selection of which are on public display
during normal weekday hours when the
university is in session. Online gallery also
available.

The Costume Institute
The Metropolitan Museum of Art
1000 Fifth Avenue at 82nd Street
New York, NY 10028-0198
Tel: 212-535-7710
Email: thecostumeinstitute@metmuseum.org
Website: www.metmuseum.org
Vast collection of 80,000 costumes.

The Kent State University Museum
PO Box 5190
Rockwell Hall
Kent, OH 44242-0001
Tel: 330-672-3450
Email: museum@kent.edu
Website: www.kent.edu/museum
A collection of mainly twentieth-century
garments, representing the work of most
major American and European designers,
including some of their archives and sketch-
books. Stages exhibitions from its collection.

Vintage Fashion Museum
212 N. Broadway
Abilene, KS 67410
Tel: 785-263-7997
Email: fashion@ikansas.com
Website: www.abilenekansas.org
Fashions from the 1870s to the 1970s.

CANADA

Costume Museum of Canada
Box 38
Dugald, Manitoba
Tel: 1-204-853-2166
Toll-free: 866-853-2166
Email: info@costumemuseum.com
Website: costumemuseum.com
Intended as a national repository for
costume, textiles, and accessories, the
collection includes designs by Chanel,
Norman Hartnell, Worth, Schiaparelli,
Vionnet, Scassi, and Paco Rabanne.

AUSTRALIA

Powerhouse Museum
500 Harris Street Ultimo
PO Box K346
Haymarket, Sydney
New South Wales 1238
Tel: (+61) 2-9217-0111
Website: www.powerhousemuseum.com
Occasional exhibitions of contemporary
and vintage fashion and style icons, such
as Audrey Hepburn.

Stores and Boutiques

UNITED KINGDOM

Appleby
95 Westbourne Park Villas
London W2 5ED
Tel: (+44) 207-229-7772
Email: jane@applebyvintage.com
Website: www.applebyvintage.com
Friendly and accommodating vintage
boutique run by Jane Appleby.

Blackout II
51 Endell Street
London WC2 9HJ
Tel: (+44) 207-240-5006
Email: clothes@blackout2.com
Website: www.blackout2.com
Specializes in clothing from the 1930s
and 1940s.

Cenci
4 Nettlefold Place
London SE27 0JW
Tel: (+44) 020 8766 8564
Email: info@cenci.co.uk
Website: www.cenci.co.uk
Vintage fashion and accessories from
the 1930s onward.

C20 Vintage Fashion
Email: enquiries@c20vintagefashion.co.uk
Website: www.c20vintagefashion.co.uk
Cleo and Mark Butterfield's inspirational
vintage garments are available for hire.

Decades
17-18 Dover Street
London W1S 4LT
Tel: (+44) 207-518-0680
Email: info@decadesinc.com
Website: www.decadesinc.com

One of a Kind
253 Portobello Road
London W11 1LR
Tel: (+44) 207-792-5284

Palette London
21 Canonbury Lane
London N1 2AS
Eclectic selection of vintage clothing.
Also a finder service.

Pop Boutique
6 Monmouth Street
London WC2H 9HB
Tel: (+44) 207-497-5262
Email: info@pop-boutique.com
Website: www.madaboutpop.com
1960s, 1970s, and 1980s originals as well
as its own retro pop label.

Rellik
8 Golborne Road
London W10 5NW
Tel: (+44) 208-962-0089
Website: www.relliklondon.co.uk
Clothing and accessories from the
1920s to mid-1980s.

Rokit
42 Shelton Street
Covent Garden
London WC2H 9HZ
Tel: (+44) 207-836-6547
Website: www.rokit.co.uk

Steinberg & Tolkien
193 King's Road
London SW3 5ED
Tel: (+44) 207-376-3660
Well-established shop owned by
Tracy Tolkien selling vintage clothing,
accessories, and jewelry.

The Vintage Clothing Company
Afflecks Palace
Oldham Street
Manchester M4 1PW
Tel: (+44) 161-832-0548
Website: www.vintageclothingcompany.com
Part of a chain of five retail outlets.

Virginia
98 Portland Road
London W11 4LQ
Tel: (+44) 207-727-9908
Exquisite antique clothing.

UNITED STATES
Decades
8214½ Melrose Avenue
Los Angeles, CA 90046
Tel: 323-655-0223
Website: www.decadesinc.com
Fabulous collection by Cameron Silver, who
has now opened his second shop in London.

Keni Valenti Retro-Couture
155 West 29th Street
Third floor, Room C5
New York, NY 10001
Tel: 212-967-7147
Website: www.kenivalenti.com

The Paper Bag Princess
8818 Olympic Boulevard
Beverly Hills, CA 90211
Tel: 310-385-9036
Website: www.thepaperbagprincess.com

William Doyle Galleries
175 East 87th Street
New York, NY 10128
Tel: 212-427-2730
Email: info@DoyleNewYork.com
Website: www.doylegalleries.com
Auctioneers and appraisers of
haute couture and antique costume.

CANADA
Deluxe Junk Company
310 W. Cordova Street
Vancouver, British Columbia V6B 1E8
Tel: 1-604-685-4871
Email: dlxjunk@telus.net
Website: www.deluxejunk.com
Vancouver's oldest vintage clothing store.
Great selection of vintage and contemporary
clothing, accessories, and costume jewelry.

MaryAnn Harris
Ottawa Antique Market
1179 Bank Street
Ottawa, Ontario
Tel: 1-613 720 9242

AUSTRALIA
Vintage Clothing Shop
147–49 Castlereagh Street
Shop 5, CBD
Sydney 2000

Organizations
Costume Society
www.costumesociety.org.uk
The society includes collectors, curators,
designers, lecturers, students, and informed
enthusiasts with the aim to explore all
aspects of clothing history.

Costume Society of America
www.costumesocietyamerica.com
Dedicated to the history and conservation of
dress adornment and to interpreting culture
through appearance.

Vintage Fashion Guild
www.vintagefashionguild.org
An online resource set up by a collective
of vintage sellers. Offers information, news,
and a virtual museum, plus guidance for
vintage costume vendors.

Online stores
www.antiquedress.com
www.antique-fashion.com
www.shockadelic.com
www.thefrock.com
www.tias.com/stores/decades
www.unique-vintage.com
www.vintageblues.com
www.vintagemartini.com
www.vintagetextile.com
www.vintagetrends.com
www.vintagevixen.com

Fashion websites
www.costumegallery.com
www.costumes.org
www.fabrics.net
www.fashionencyclopedia.com
www.fashion-era.com
www.pastpatterns.com
www.vpll.org

Glossary of Designers

Adolfo (1933-): Bergdorf Goodman; Emme; Adolfo

Adrian, Gilbert (1903-59): Paramount; Adrian Limited

Agnès, Madame (1910-40): Madame Agnès millinery

Alaïa, Azzedine (1940-): Christian Dior; Guy Laroche;
Azzedine Alaïa

Amies, Sir Hardy (1909-2003): Lachasse; Hardy Amies

Armani, Giorgio (1934-): Nino Cerruti; Giorgio Armani

Ashley, Laura (1925-85): Laura Ashley

Augustabernard: Founded by Augusta Bernard in 1919

Bakst, Léon (1866-1924): Ballets Russes

Balenciaga, Cristóbal (1895-1972): Balenciaga couture house

Balmain, Pierre (1914-82): Robert Piguet; Edward Molyneux;
Lucien Lelong; Balmain

Banton, Travis (1894-1958): Lucile Duff Gordon; Paramount;
Twentieth-Century Fox; Universal Studios

Bates, John (1935-): Herbert Sidon; Jean Varon; John Bates

Beene, Geoffrey (1927-): Teal Traina; Geoffrey Beene, Inc.;
Beenebag

Berardi, Antonio (1968-): Antonio Berardi

Biagiotti, Laura (1943-): Roberto Cappuci, Laura Biagiotti

Biba: Founded by Barbara Hulanicki (1936-) in 1964

Bikkembergs, Dirk (1962-): Freelance designer for Nero, Bassetti,
Gruno and Chardin, Tiktiner, Gaffa, K, and Jaco Petti;
Dirk Bikkembergs

Birtwell, Celia (1941-): Ossie Clark and others;
Celia Birtwell, London

Blass, Bill (1922-2002): Anna Miller and Company; Maurice Retner;
Bill Blass Limited

Bodymap: Founded by David Holah and Stevie Stewart in 1982

Bohan, Marc (1926-): Jean Patou; Robert Piguet;
Edward Molyneux; Patou; Christian Dior; Hartnell

Boué Soeurs, House of: Founded by Jeanne Boué in 1899

Bruce, Liza (1955-): Liza Bruce

Burrows, Stephen (1943-): Stephen Burrows' World

Byblos: Founded in 1973

Cacharel, Jean (1932-): Jean Jourdan; Société Jean Cacharel

Callot Soeurs, House of: Founded by the Callot sisters
in 1895

Capucci, Roberto (1929-): Emilio Schuberth; Roberto Capucci

Cardin, Pierre (1922-): Madam Paquin; Elsa Schiaparelli; Christian
Dior; Pierre Cardin

Carnegie, Hattie (1889-1956): Macy's; Hattie Carnegie Originals;
Hattie Carnegie

Cashin, Bonnie (1915-2000): Adler and Adler;
Twentieth-Century Fox; Bonnie Cashin Designs

Cassini, Oleg (1913-): Jean Patou; Edith Head; Oleg Cassini;
Jacqueline Kennedy

Castelbajac Jean-Charles de (1949-): André Courrèges;
Jean-Charles de Castelbajac

Cavanagh, John (1914-): Edward Molyneux; Pierre Balmain;
John Cavanagh

Céline: Founded in 1973

Cerruti, Nino (1930-): Nino Cerruti

Chalayan, Hussein (1970-): Cartesia Ltd.; Hussein Chalayan

Chanel, Gabrielle "Coco" (1883-1971): House of Chanel

Chéruit, Madeleine: Founded by Madeleine Chéruit in 1900

Chloé: Founded by Gaby Aghion and Jacques Lanoir in 1952

Clark, Ossie (1942-96): Quorum; Radley; Evocative

Clergerie, Robert (1934-): Charles Jourdan;
Clerma Company; J. Fenestrier

Colonna, Jean (1955-): Balmain; Jean Colonna

Comme des Garçons: Founded by Rei Kawakubo (1942-) in 1973

Connolly, Sybil (1921-98): Bradleys; Richard Alan;
Sybil Connolly Inc.; Tiffany's

Courrèges, André (1923-): Jeanne Laufrie; Cristóbal Balenciaga;
André Courrèges

Crahay, Jules François (1917-88): Nina Ricci; Jeanne Lanvin

Creed, Charles Southey (1909-66): Linton Tweeds; Bergdorf Goodman;
Charles Creed

Daché, Lilly (1907-89): Reboux; Macy's; The Bonnet Shop;
Travis Banton

De la Renta, Oscar (1932-): Cristóbal Balenciaga; Lanvin;
Oscar de la Renta

De Lisi, Ben (1955-): Saks; Penelope; Benedetto; Ben de Lisi

De Prémonville, Myrène (1949-): Myrène de Prémonville

Delaunay, Sonia (1885-1979): Abstract painter and designer

Demeulemeester, Ann (1959-): Ann Demeulemeester

Dessès, Jean (1904-70): Jean Dessès; Jean Dessès American Collection

Dior, Christian (1905-57): Robert Piguet; Lelong; Maison Dior;
House of Christian Dior

Doeuillet, House of: Founded by Georges Doeuillet in 1900

Dolce & Gabbana: Founded by Domenico Dolce and
Stefano Gabbana in 1985

Doucet, Jacques (1853-1929): Maison Doucet

Duff Gordon, Lucille (1862-1935): Lucile couture house

Edelstein, Victor (1947-): Alexon; Biba; Christian Dior; Victor Edelstein

Elbaz, Albert (1961-): Geoffrey Beene; Guy Laroche; YSL Rive Gauche

Ellis, Perry (1940-86): Miller & Rhoads; Perry Ellis International

Emanuel, David (1952-) and Elizabeth (1953-): Emanuel

Erté (Romaine de Tirtoff 1892-1990): Costume designs
for ballet and theater

Estrada, Angel (1957-89): Estrada

Ettedgui, Joseph (1936-): Chain of shops including Joseph,
Joseph Tricot, Joseph Pour La Maison

Fath, Jacques (1912-54): Jacques Fath couture house

Fendi: Founded by Adele Casagrande in 1918

Féraud, Louis (1921-99): Louis Féraud

Ferragamo, Salvatore (1898-1960): Bonito;
    Salvatore Ferragamo

Ferré, Gianfranco (1944-): Gianfranco Ferré Donna;
    Christian Dior; Gianfranco Ferré

Ferretti, Alberta (1950-): Aeffe

Fiorucci, Elio: Founded by Elio Fiorucci in 1962

Flett, John (1963-91): Lanvin; Enrico Coveri

Foale & Tuffin: Founded by Marion Foale and
    Sally Tuffin in 1961

Ford, Tom (1962-): Cathy Harwick; Perry Ellis; Gucci;
    YSL Rive Gauche

Fortuny, Mariano (1871-1949): Fortuny couture house

Fox, Frederick (1931-): Otto Lucas; Mitzi Lorenz; Langée;
    Frederick Fox

Fratini, Gina (1934-): Katherine Dunham dance group;
    Hartnell; Gina Fratini

Galanos, James (1924-): Hattie Carnegie; Robert Piguet; Davidow;
    Galanos Originals

Galliano, John (1960-) John Galliano; Givenchy; Christian Dior

Gaultier, Jean Paul (1952-): Pierre Cardin; Esterel; Jean Patou;
    Jean Paul Gaultier SA

Gernreich, Rudi (1922-85): Lester Horton Dance Company;
    William Bass; GR Designs; Rudi Gernreich, Inc.

Gibb, Bill (1943-88): Baccarat; Bill Gibb Fashion Group

Gigli, Romeo (1949-): Dimitri Couture; Romeo Gigli

Givenchy, Hubert de (1927-): Jaques Fath; Robert Piguet;
    Lucien Lelong; Elsa Schiaparelli; Maison Givenchy

Godley, Georgina (1955-): Crolla; Georgina Godley Ltd.

Greer, Howard (1896-1974): Paul Poiret; Edward Molyneux;
    Paramount; Howard Greer

Grès, Madame (1903-93): Premet; Alix; Grès

Griffe, Jacques (1917-): Vionnet; Edward Molyneux,
    Jacques Griffe

Gucci, Guccio (1881-1953): Gucci

Halston, Roy Frowick (1932-90): Lilly Daché; Bergdorf Goodman;
    Halston Ltd.

Hamnett, Katharine (1948-): Tuttabanken Sportswear;
    Katharine Hamnett Ltd.

Hartnell, Sir Norman (1901-79): Madame Desirée;
    Norman Hartnell

Head, Edith (1907-81): Paramount Studios; Universal Studios

Heim, Jacques (1899-1967): Jacques Heim

Hermès: Founded by Thierry Hermès in 1837

Howell, Margaret (1946-): Margaret Howell

Jackson, Betty (1949-): Quorum Design Studio; Betty Jackson

Jacobs, Marc (1964-): Ruben Thomas, Inc.; Perry Ellis;
    Marc Jacobs; Louis Vuitton

James, Charles (1906-78): E Haweis James; Charles James

Johnson, Betsey (1942-): Paraphernalia Boutiques; Betsey, Bunky
    & Nini; Alvin Duskin Co.; Alley Cat; Betsey Johnson; BJ Vines

Jones, Stephen (1957-): Fiorucci; Stephen Jones

Kamali, Norma (1945-): Kamili; OMO Norma Kamali boutiques

Karan, Donna (1948-): Anne Klein; Donna Karan; DKNY

Kelly, Patrick (1954-90): Le Palais club; Patrick Kelly, Paris

Kenzo (1939-): Freelance designer to Féraud; Rodier; Pisanti;
    Jungle Jap; Kenzo

Keogh, Lainey (1957-): Lainey Keogh

Kerrigan, Daryl (1964-): Daryl Kerrigan

Khanh, Emmanuelle (1937-): Cacharel; Dorothée Bis;
    Emmanuelle Khanh

Klein, Anne (1923-74): Varden Petites; Anne Klein

Klein, Calvin (1942-): Dan Millstein; Calvin Klein Co.

Kors, Michael (1959-): Michael Kors; Céline

Krizia: founded by Mariuccia Mandelli in 1954

Lachasse, House of: Founded in 1928

Lacroix, Christian (1951-): Hermès; Guy Paulin; Jean Patou;
    Christian Lacroix

Lagerfeld, Karl (1938-): Balmain; Patou; Chloé; Krizia; Chanel

Lang, Helmut (1956-): Helmut Lang

Lanvin, Jeanne (1867-1946): Jeanne Lanvin couture house

Lapidus, Ted (1929-): Ted Lapidus

Laroche, Guy (1923-89): Jean Dessès; Guy Laroche couture house

Lauren, Ralph (1939-): Polo Fashions; Polo Ralph Lauren

Léger, Hervé (1957-): Fendi; Chanel; Lanvin; Chloé;
    Charles Jourdan; Hervé Léger

Lelong, Lucien (1889-1958): House of Lelong

Lesage: Founded by Albert Lesage in 1868

Lester, Charles & Patricia: Founded by Charles and Patricia
    Lester in 1964

Liberty: Founded by Arthur Lasenby in 1875

Loewe: Founded by Enrique Loewe in 1846

Louiseboulanger: Founded by Louise Boulanger in 1927

Lucas, Otto (1903-71): Otto Lucas

McCardell, Claire (1905-58): Emmet Joyce; Robert Turk;
    Townley Frocks; Hattie Carnegie

McFadden, Mary (1938-): Mary McFadden

Mackie, Bob (1940-): Cole of California, Bob Mackie Originals

Mainbocher (1890-1976): Mainbocher couture house

Margiela, Martin (1957-): Jean Paul Gaultier; Martin Margiela

Matsuda, Mitsuhiro (1934-): Nicole Limited; Matsuda

MaxMara: Founded by Achille Maramotti in 1951;
    encompasses 16 labels

Missoni: Founded by Ottavio and Rosita Missoni in 1953

Miyake, Issey (1938-): Laroche; Givenchy; Geoffrey Beene;
    Issey Miyake

Mizrahi, Isaac (1961-): Perry Ellis; Calvin Klein; Isaac Mizrahi

Model, Philippe (1956-): shoes and accessories –
  worked with Gaultier, Claude Montana, Issey Miyake;
  Thierry Mugler

Molinari, Anna (1948): Blumarine

Molyneux, Captain Edward (1891-1974): Lucile; Molyneux

Montana, Claude (1949-): Idéal-Cuir; MacDougal Leathers;
  Lanvin

Morton, Digby (1906-83): Digby Morton

Moschino, Franco (1950-94): Gianni Versace; Cadette;
  Moschino

Mugler, Thierry (1948-): Gudule boutique; André Peters;
  Thierry Mugler

Muir, Jean (1928-95): Jacqmar; Jaeger; Courtaulds;
  Jane & Jane; Jean Muir Ltd.

Norell, Norman (1900-72): Brooks Costume Company;
  Charles Amour; Hattie Carnegie; Triana-Norell

Nutter, Tommy (1943-92): Donaldson, Williams & Ward;
  Tommy Nutter; Austin Reed

Oldfield, Bruce (1950-): Bruce Oldfield Ltd.

Oldham, Todd (1961-): L-7; Todd Oldham

Orry-Kelly, John (1898-1964): Costume design for Warner
  Brothers; Twentieth-Century Fox; Universal Studios; MGM

Ozbek, Rifat (1953-): Trell; Monsoon; Ozbek; Future Ozbek

Paquin: Founded by Jeanne Beckers and Isidore Jacobs in 1891

Patou, Jean (1880-1936): Jean Patou

Pertegaz, Manuel (1918-): Manuel Pertegaz

Piguet, Robert (1901-53): Paul Poiret; John Redfern;
  Robert Piguet

Plunkett, Walter (1902-82): RKO; MGM

Poiret, Paul (1879-1947): Charles Worth; Jacques Doucet;
  Paul Poiret

Porter, Thea (1927-2000): Thea Porter

Prada: Founded by Mario Prada in 1913

Price, Antony (1945-): Stirling Cooper; Plaza; Antony Price

Pucci, Marchese Emilio (1914-92): Lord & Taylor; Pucci

Quant, Mary (1934-): Bazaar; Mary Quant Ginger Group

Rabanne, Paco (1934-): Givenchy; Dior; Balenciaga;
  Paco Rabanne

Reboux, Caroline (1830-1927): Vionnet; Caroline Reboux

Redfern: Founded by John Redfern in 1881

Rhodes, Zandra (1940-): Zandra Rhodes Ltd.

Ricci, Nina (1883-1970): Nina Ricci couture house

Rocha, John (1953-): John Rocha

Rodriquez, Narciso (1961-): Calvin Klein; Cerruti; Loewe

Rouff, Maggy (1896-1971): Drécoll; Maggy Rouff

Rykiel, Sonia (1930-): Laura Boutique; Sonia Rykiel

Saint Laurent, Yves (1936-): Christian Dior; Yves Saint Laurent;
  YSL Rive Gauche

Sander, Jil (1943-): Jil Sander

Sant'Angelo, Giorgio di (1936-89): Sant'Angelo

Sassoon, Bellville: Founded by Belinda Bellville and David Sassoon in 1958

Scaasi, Arnold (1931-): Jeanne Paquin; Lilly Daché; Charles James; Arnold Scaasi

Scherrer, Jean-Louis (1936-): Christian Dior; Yves Saint Laurent;
  Louis Féraud; Jean-Louis Scherrer

Schiaparelli, Elsa (1890-1973): House of Schiaparelli – worked
  with Salvador Dalí, Christian Bérard; Jean Cocteau

Schön, Mila (1919-): Mila Schön

Sharaff, Irene (1910-93): Aline Bernstein; MGM

Sitbon, Martine (1951-): Chloé; Martine Sitbon

Sprouse, Stephen (1953-): Halston; Bill Blass; Stephen Sprouse

Stiebel, Victor (1907-76): Reville; Rossiter; Victor Stiebel; Jacqmar

Sui, Anna (1955-): Simultanee; Anna Sui

Tarlazzi, Angelo (1942-): Carosa; Patou; Angelo Tarlazzi; Guy Laroche

Thomass, Chantal (1947-): Dorothée Bis; Chantal Thomass

Trigère, Pauline (1912-2002): Hattie Carnegie; Pauline Trigère

Tyler, Richard (1946-): Anne Klein; Byblos; Richard Tyler Couture;
  Richard Tyler Collection

Ungaro, Emanuel (1933-): Cristóbal Balenciaga; André Courrèges;
  Emanuel Ungaro couture house

Valentino (1932-): Jean Dessès; Guy Laroche; Valentino

Vanderbilt, Gloria (1924-): Gloria Vanderbilt

Van Noten, Dries (1958-): Dries Van Noten

Versace, Gianni (1946-97): Callaghan; Genny; Complice; Gianni Versace

Vionnet, Madeleine (1876-1975): House of Vincent; Kate Reilly;
  Callot Soeurs; Jacques Doucet; House of Vionnet

Vittadini, Adrienne (1944-): Louis Féraud; Sport Tempo; Warnaco;
  Kimberly Knits; Adrienne Vittadini

von Furstenberg, Diane (1946-): Diane von Furstenberg Studio;
  Diane von Furstenberg couture house

Walker, Catherine (1945-): Chelsea Design Company

Watanabe, Junya (1961-): Rei Kawakubo

Westwood, Vivienne (1941-): Vivienne Westwood

Workers for Freedom: Founded by Richard Nott and
  Graham Fraser in 1985

Worth, Charles Frederick (1825-95): House of Worth

Yamamoto, Kansai (1944-): Junko Koshino; Hisashi Hosono;
  Yamamoto Kansai Company Ltd.

Yamamoto, Yohji (1943-): Yohji Yamamoto

Yuki (1937-): Louis Féraud; Michael Donellan; Norman Hartnell;
  Pierre Cardin; Yuki

Zoran (1947-): Zoran

Glossary of Fashion Terms

Acetate: based on cellulose, this chemical fiber was first manufactured in 1864 and has been in mass production since 1920.

Ajouré: collective description of fine open-work, embroidered fabric.

A-line: created by Christian Dior, A-line describes a dress shaped in outline like the letter A. From narrow shoulders and a low waist, it flares out to a wide skirt.

American shoulder: an armhole obliquely cut to reveal the shoulder.

Argyll (also Argyle): often seen on woolen socks and sweaters, this diamond pattern was named after an area of western Scotland.

Armani sleeves: turned-up sleeves created from two different fabrics.

Baker's check: similar in pattern to gingham, but twice the size.

Ballerina length: hem length that falls just above the ankles.

Balloon skirt: wide skirt hemmed to curve inward at the knees. Fashionable in cocktail dresses until 1958; enjoyed a revival in the late 1980s and again as part of the late 1990s retro look.

Balloon sleeve: created in 1890, this very full sleeve is held in place by a cuff at the wrist. Later revived by Nina Ricci.

Bateau neck: also known as a boatneck, this is a collarless, boat-shaped neckline that runs from shoulder to shoulder.

Batwing sleeve: set deep and wide in the armhole, this sleeve tapers toward a tight wrist.

Besom pocket: a pocket sewn inside the garment with a slit welt opening.

Bias cut: a technique of cutting across the grain of the fabric, introduced in the 1920s by Madeleine Vionnet.

Blouson: a style (such as a dress, blouse, or jacket) having a full bodice gathered or pleated into a close-fitting waistband.

Body stocking: close-fitting, one-piece garment of elastic material covering the whole body.

Bolero: open, waist- (or above) length jacket adopted from Spanish costume.

Bomber jacket: military-style blouson jacket, usually made of nylon.

Bord-à-bord jacket: women's jacket in which the front edges abut rather than cross. Held together with toggles or frogs, etc.

Boule shape: similar to Paul Poiret's hobble skirt, this is a skirt that is full below the waist, becoming tighter at the hem.

Box skirt: a straight skirt with a waistband and two thick, often quilted monk's seams running along the front and back.

Bustier: corsetlike, strapless top of variable length above the waist. First worn as undergarments, bustiers are now worn as outerwear.

Bustle: pad or hoops used as a base over which the rear of a skirt is draped to emphasize the derriere. First in fashion around 1785, it was later adapted by Christian Dior and more recently by Vivienne Westwood.

Caftan: loosely cut, straight ankle-length dress.

Camel hair: soft, short undercoat of the camel from which a soft, woolen fabric is made.

Capri pants: narrow, three-quarter-length ladies' trousers with a small slit at the side of the hem. Created by Emilio Pucci in the 1950s, capri pants were inspired by trousers worn by Italian fishermen.

Casaque: fashionable in the 1920s, 1930s, and 1950s, this hip-length blouse is worn over a skirt or as a jumper over trousers around 1965–70.

Cascade neckline: a neckline consisting of narrow straps and a cascade of fabric at the front.

Cashmere: the hair of the Kashmir goat is used to make a soft light wool.

Cauterization: acid is applied to a blended fabric to destroy part of one of the types of fiber and creates a pattern – for example, devoré velvet.

Chalk stripes: pale stripes set on a dark background but less defined and spaced wider apart than pin stripes.

Chantilly lace: fine black bobbin lace, often with baroque or rococo-style motifs or swags of flowers.

Chasuble pleat: a pleat covering the top seams of sleeves, it broadens the appearance of the shoulders.

Chauffe-coeur: sleeved undershirt created from warm fabric with a low-cut, round neck. Barely waist-length, it was adapted from ballet clothes.

Chenille: cut in the warp of a fabric, the fibers of this yarn stand proud and produce an effect similar to velvet. Chenille yarn is used to make corduroy and velour, also terry cloth and carpets.

Chiffon: translucent, light fabric with a matte surface made from synthetic fibers or natural silk.

Circular skirt: based on a circular or semicircular cut, this skirt is narrow at the hips and frequently supported by godets.

Cocktail dress: a short dress, often with a low neckline. Suitable for a variety of occasions when worn with a bolero or short jacket, this dress dates back to the 1940s.

Color blocking: contrasting expanses of color on fabric give clothes a graphic quality, as in Courrèges designs.

Corsair pants: narrow trousers cut slightly wider than capri pants, with slits below the knees.

Cossack pants: ankle- or calf-length trousers, baggy with a wide waist held by a belt.

Cowl neck: this wide, cylindrical piece of fabric tubing is attached to the neck of a garment.

Crepe: heat and a crêpe weave give this fabric its wrinkled surface.

Crepe de chine: made from natural or synthetic silk, this is a delicate, sheer fabric with a crinkled surface.

Crinoline: originally made of horsehair, later steel hoops held together with fabric tape, this rigid petticoat gave width to skirts. Reappeared in Vivienne Westwood's mini-crinis in the 1980s.

Cup collar: open at the front, this stand-up collar is set at the back so the fabric falls in cuplike arches.

Cutout: an area cut out of a garment.

Diana décolleté: first seen in the second half of the nineteenth century, this asymmetrical neckline featured one bare shoulder. In the 1930s it was adopted by Elsa Schiaparelli and then later by Madam Grès in the 1950s; it regained popularity in the late 1970s.

Dior vent or Dior pleat: a short vent created for Christian Dior's 1948 tight pencil skirt.

Dirndl: this full skirt is gathered into the waistband.

Dolman sleeve: cut as an extension of the bodice, this sleeve was probably copied from a Turkish robe. Emanuel Ungaro created an angular version, known as the Ungaro dolman, in 1968.

Empire line: dresses and coats are gathered beneath the bust and fall loosely to the feet. This style frequently comes back in fashion.

Encrustment: fabric pieces, such as leather, lace, or trimmings, inserted into another yet distinct from appliqué.

Epaulet: originally designed to prevent slippage of shoulder-slung rifles and later a symbol of rank, this shoulder piece gives a military touch to clothes. It first appeared in female fashions in the 1930s.

Flapper dress: fashionable in the 1920s, this dress featured narrow shoulder straps and a low waist, often tied with a scarf or belt.

Folkloric: dress style that assimilates elements of national costumes from around the world.

French cuffs: double cuffs.

French pocket: a pocket set in the side seams of a skirt or trousers.

Garçonne: severe, masculine style of dress of the 1920s.

Gaucho pants: wide-bottomed, calf-length trousers based on those worn by South American cowboys (gauchos); fashionable in the early 1970s.

Georgette crepe: translucent crêpe fabric.

Gigot, or leg-of-mutton, sleeve: tight-fitting from cuffed wrist to elbow, this sleeve puffs up from elbow to shoulder.

Godet: sewn into a skirt, this triangular piece of fabric is designed to produce fullness.

Greatcoat reverse: named after the lapel on a greatcoat, which is produced by undoing the top button, this is a wide lapel.

Halter-neck: top or dress with straps tied at the nape of the neck to leave the back and shoulders exposed.

Herringbone: produced by a broken twill weave and often emphasized with yarns in a variety of colors, this diagonally lined pattern resembles the skeleton of a herring.

H-line: launched by Christian Dior in 1954-55, this slightly tailored line has a slender top and narrow hips.

Hobble skirt: created by Paul Poiret in 1910, this ankle-length skirt is cut and draped to narrow beneath the knee, allowing only small steps to be taken.

Houndstooth: traditional small check pattern of two colors, often black and white. Due to the pattern linking individual checks, it is distinguishable from pepita (*see page 219*).

I-line: a narrow line silhouette created by Cristóbal Balenciaga in 1954-55.

Jabot: used to cover buttons on dresses or blouses, this decorative ruffle became popular with women from the late nineteenth century until the late 1950s, and then became fashionable once more in a modified form in 1980.

Jersey: a knitted fabric that feels soft to the touch and is pliable without losing its shape; first introduced in haute couture by Coco Chanel in 1916-17.

Jodhpurs: riding breeches that are narrow on the calves and very full from hip to knee. Since the 1970s they have enjoyed various revivals.

Jumper: collarless sleeveless dress based on a chasuble.

Jumpsuit: one-piece pantsuit usually made of an elastic material such as jersey and with long or short legs. Introduced in the 1960s.

Kangaroo pocket: often seen on the front of cagoules, this is a large patch pocket.

Kimono sleeve: as in the Japanese kimono, this is a straight sleeve that is joined at right angles to a garment.

Knickers: loose, full breeches gathered beneath the knee, but more narrow than plus fours; revived in the 1960s.

Lamé: fabric that is interwoven with metallic threads.

Leggings: footless leg covering created from elastic material; popular in the 1980s.

Liberty: British fashion and textile firm famous for its cotton floral prints

Louver pleats: pleats running horizontally.

Mandarin (or Chinese, or Nehru) collar: stand-up collar that is open at the front.

Maxiskirt: ankle- or floor-length skirt popular around 1970.

Midiskirt: calf-length skirt; although this term is no longer in use, the length itself has been dominant since 1973.

Military style: often in khaki, this look is inspired by military uniforms.

Miniskirt: a very short skirt, with the minimum distance between hem and knee being 4 inches.

Moiré: generally used for formal eveningwear, this is a watered effect on fabric; formerly silk, now also acetate.

Nautical style: leisure- and sportswear style, usually in navy blue and white, and modeled on naval uniforms.

New Look (Corolla line): world-famous silhouette created in 1947 by Christian Dior. Very feminine, with narrow, rounded shoulders, narrow waist, emphasized bust and wide, calf-length skirt.

Nylon: patented in the U.S. in 1937 and initially used in the manufacture of hosiery and underwear.

Op art: art style typified by abstract, geometric patterns and bold colors, especially black and white; a major influence in 1960s fashion.

Organdy: lightweight, sheer stiffened cotton (now often synthetic), usually in pastel shades.

Organza: similar to organdy, this fabric was originally made of silk.

Oversized look: garments that appear several sizes too large; fashionable in the 1980s.

Pagoda shoulder: launched in 1933 by Elsa Schiaparelli, this emphasized shoulder was inspired by Asian pagodas.

Paletot: single- or double-breasted coat with patch pockets and lapels.

Panniers: structured undergarment or hoops that extended the width of the dress to both sides while leaving the front and back flat. Popular in the eighteenth century, modified versions have appeared since then.

Parallelo: very fashionable in the 1950s, this is a horizontally knitted sweater or jacket.

Passementerie: generic term for all kinds of garment (and furnishing) trimmings, essential requirements for Coco Chanel's suits.

Passe-partout jacket: similar to a bolero.

Pencil line: figure-hugging style created by Christian Dior in 1948, whereby the skirt is cut from the hips in one straight line.

Pennant collar: triangular-shaped collar.

Pepita: small, checked, and woven pattern with diagonal connecting lines, usually in navy and white or black and white.

Peplum jacket: short tailored jacket with flared flaps or flounces sewn into the waist.

Peter Pan collar: rounded, small flat collar.

Piqué: cotton fabric with a relief pattern; it is usually waffled or honeycombed.

Plissé: term used to describe pleats that are pressed into fabric.

Princess line: coat or dress without a waist seam; tailoring is achieved by working in the vertical seam. It was launched in 1863 by Charles Frederick Worth, was popular again in 1900, in the 1930s, and then again between 1955 and 1965.

Puff sleeve: gathered above the elbow, this is a balloonlike short sleeve.

Puffball, or pouf, skirt: created by Christian Lacroix in the 1980s, the skirt is doubled over at the hem to create a puffed appearance.

Pullover: knitted garment pulled on over the head, inspired by the knitted garments worn by seamen. Popular in 1920s Europe, when Coco Chanel included it in several of her haute couture collections.

Raglan sleeve: a sleeve extending from the neckline to the wrist.

Rayon: a name for viscose used between the early 1950s and the 1970s.

Redingote: tailored long jacket or coat, usually flared toward the hem and often with a shawl collar. It can be worn with or without a belt.

Revers: lapels; can refer to the turned-over edge of sleeves or skirts.

Romantic look: 1960s and 1970s style of dress, incorporating folk elements and featuring loose cotton dresses, ruffles, and corset tops.

Sabrina neckline: inspired by Audrey Hepburn's clothes in the movie of the same name, this is a square, décolleté collar.

Safari jacket: jacket in a strong, lightweight fabric, which is modeled on tropical garments. It is characterized by the colors brown, beige, and khaki, and by patch pockets and shoulder flaps. Usually fitted with a belt.

Sailor collar: neckline and collar inspired by naval uniforms.

Sailor neck: zipper-fastened turtleneck.

Shantung: irregular, less shiny silk; handwoven.

Sheath dress: usually knee-length classic dress, collarless and close-fitting, straight and cut from a single fabric piece, with a round or oval neckline; also an evening dress with shoulder straps and décolletage; popular in the 1920s, in the 1960s it became known as the "Jackie O. dress" (after Jacqueline Kennedy).

Shelf bra: a bra that is built into the garment.

Shift dress: loosely falling, unstructured classic style of dress especially fashionable during the 1920s and mid-1960s.

Shirtwaister: the upper part of this loose dress is modeled on a man's shirt, with a collar, cuffs, and buttons to the waist. Popularized by Coco Chanel.

Slinky look: originally fashionable in the 1930s and later revived in the early 1970s; a phrase used to describe sinuous clothes of fluid fabrics.

Slit look: a miniskirt or hot pants worn beneath a midi- or maxiskirt left open at the front; fashionable in the early 1970s.

Smock: narrow straight dress with front, back, and sleeves secured to a yoke collar.

Smocking: fabric tightly gathered with decorative stitching (often created with elastic thread) to form geometric patterns; frequently featured in peasant-style garments.

Spencer: waist-length short jacket.

Sportswear: generic term to describe comfortable leisurewear.

Swing coat: style of A-line coat, with narrow sleeves and shoulders; shorter than knee-length.

Taffeta: stiffened fine fabric of synthetic fibers or silk often made of *changeant* (an iridescent material).

Tea gown: loose gown designed in 1864 by Charles Frederick Worth with an intricately decorated front and long sleeves.

Topper: straight short jacket with sloping shoulders, the front edge forms a right angle with the hem.

Torso dress: simple dress that is gathered or pleated below the hipline with a figure-hugging bodice.

Trapeze line: silhouette of coat or dress with narrow shoulders and a high waist (or no waist at all) flaring out toward the hem. Yves Saint Laurent presented his Trapeze line in 1958, and it remained popular through the 1960s.

Tube: garment with a straight, elongated outline, which is cut in a casual and comfortable way.

Tulle: a fine net fabric, traditionally silk.

Tunic: simple jumper or dress in a loose, often sleeveless style; the armholes usually form part of the side seams.

Tweed: rough-textured woolen fabric in a variety of colored patterns; used especially for suits and coats.

Twist line: narrow-hipped outline with a slightly flared pleated skirt that flares as the wearer moves around.

Umbrella skirt: like an umbrella, this skirt consists of 12 or more sections.

U-neckline: neckline in a U-shape with wide shoulder straps.

V-neck: neckline with an open yoke coming to a V shape midway down the bodice.

Velvet: soft-textured, short-piled fabric; or silk, cotton, or synthetic fibers.

Vichy check: checked pattern that is like gingham but with larger checks.

Viennese seam: a seam running from one armhole angled across the bust to either the hem or the waist seam, obviating the need for darts.

Viscose: synthetic fiber made of cellulose.

Voile: lightweight, sheer fabric.

Westover: worn with suits in the 1920s and more recently over skirts and blouses, this is a sleeveless, knitted vest.

Wing collar: collar with upper corners covering shoulder seams.

Y-line: garment line designed in 1955–56 by Christian Dior featuring narrow dresses or skirts, wide lapels or other V-shaped necklines to form the letter *Y*.

Index

Further Reading

Aloha Attire: Hawaiian Dress in the 20th Century, Linda B. Arthur Atglen, Schiffer, 2000.

The Art of Zandra Rhodes, Zandra Rhodes/Anne Knight, Jonathan Cape, 1984.

California Casual, Maureen Reilly, P.A. Schiffer Ltd., 2001.

The Conscription of Fashion: Utility Cloth, Clothing and Footwear, 1941-1952, Christopher Sladen, Scolar Press, 1995.

The Couture Accessory, Caroline Rennolds Milbank, H.N. Abrams, 2002.

Everyday Fashions of the Thirties As Pictured in Sears Catalogs, Sears Roebuck & Company, Courier Dover Publications, 1986.

The Fashion Year, edited by Brenda Polan, Zomba Books, 1983.

The Fashion Year Volume II, edited by Emily White, Zomba Books, 1984.

Fashions of a Decade: 1940s, Patricia Baker, Batsford, 1992.

A History of Fashion, Elizabeth Ewing, Batsford, 2005.

Hollywood Costume: Glamour, Glitter & Romance, Dale McConathy with Diana Vreeland, H.N. Abrams, 1976.

Hollywood Knits, Bill Gibb, Pavilion Books, 1987.

In Biba, Delisia Howard, Chris Price and Barbara Hulanicki, Hazard Books, 2004.

In Fashion, Prudence Glynn/Madeline Ginsburg, George Allen & Unwin Ltd., 1978.

In Vogue: Sixty Years of Celebrities and Fashion from British Vogue, Georgina Howell, Penguin Books, 1978.

New York Fashion, Caroline Rennolds Milbank, H.N. Abrams, 1989.

The 1940s, John Peacock, Thames & Hudson, 1998.

NOVA 1965-1975, compiled by David Hillman and Harriet Peccinotti, edited by David Gibbs, Pavilion Books, 1993.

The Ossie Clark Diaries, Lady Henrietta Rous, Bloomsbury, 1998.

Ossie Clark 1965-74, Judith Watt, V&A Publications, 2003.

Print in Fashion, Marnie Fogg, Batsford Books, 2006.

Schiaparelli Fashion Review, Tom Tierney, Dover Publications, Inc., 1988.

Screen Style: Fashion and Femininity in 1930s Hollywood, Sarah Berry, University of Minnesota Press, 2002.

Twentieth-Century Fashion, Linda Watson, Carlton Books, 1999.

Vanitas: Designs by Gianni Versace, Hamish Bowles, Abbeville Press, 1994.

Picture Credits

The publishers would like to thank the following sources for their kind permission to reproduce the photographs in this book.

Key: t=Top, b=Bottom, c=Center, l=Left, and r=Right

The Advertising Archive Ltd.: 115, 181c

The Bridgeman Art Library: /Under the Eyes of New York Skyscrapers, fashion plate from *Femina* magazine, December 1928 (color litho), Benigni, Leon (fl.1926-29) /Private Collection, Archives Charmet: 29; /Rayon dresses designed by Lucien Lelong, fashion plate from *Femina* magazine, June 1935 (color litho), Heckroth, Pap (fl.1935) /Private Collection, Archives Charmet: 45

Camera Press: 157;/David Steen: 112

Christian Dior: 86-7

Corbis: /Michel Arnaud: 184, 193, 204; /Bettmann: 14, 34tl, 34cr, 82cl, 82tr, 110tr, 142cl, 143tr, 143bl, 147, 180cr, 196, 198; /© Condé Nast Archive: 10, 16, 20, 33, 36, 39, 40, 40 (inset), 46, 50, 53, 58cl, 60, 62, 63, 69, 70, 73, 75, 76-77, 78, 79, 82bl, 82cr, 83tr, 84, 86, 89, 92, 94, 100, 102, 103, 104-5, 105, 107, 130, 134, 136, 138-9, 150, 151, 173, 175, 179, 181cl; /Julio Donoso/Corbis Sygma: 25b, 44t, 44c, 182, 186; /Lynn Goldsmith: 206r; /Historical Picture Archive: 28; /Hulton-Deutsch Collection: 35tr, 49, 59cl, 59bl, 66, 111tr, 172; /Douglas Kirkland: 142tr; /David Lees: 110l; /Genevieve Naylor: 74, 83bl; /Philadelphia Museum of Art: 51; /Underwood & Underwood: 47; /Pierre Vauthey/Corbis Sygma: 190

Design Council Slide Collection: /Manchester Metropolitan University © Design Council, back endpaper

Getty Images: /H. Armstrong Roberts/Retrofile: 181bl; /Loomis Dean/Time Life Pictures: 99; /Pierre Guillaud/AFP: 185, 192; /Hulton Archive: 207tr; /Bill Ray/*Life* Magazine/Time & Life Pictures: p118-9; /Sasha: 58tr; /Topical Press Agency: 35c; /United Artists: 180bl; /William Vanderson/Fox Photos: 58cr

© Jim Lee: "Ossie Clark/Aeroplane 1969": 133; / " Ossie Clark/Vietnam/1969": 160

London College of Fashion: /The Woolmark Company: 127

© Niall McInerney: 188b

© Norman Parkinson Archive: 144

Réunion Musées Nationaux: /Page de contre-garde et troisième page de couverture (Titre attribué: Troisième composition) Delaunay Sonia (dit), Stern-Terk Sarah Sophie (1885-1979) © Photo CNAC/MNAM Dist. RMN - © Droits réservés: 18

Rex Features: /David Graves: 116; /Europa Press: 142cr; /Everett Collection: 111bl, 123, 142bl; /Sipa Press: 188t, 197

Roger Harris Photography: 208c, 209r, 210l, 211l and 212

TopFoto.co.uk: 35cl, 110cr, 124, 143tl, 181cr, 206l, 207bl; /AP: 111tl

Victoria & Albert Museum: /V&A Images: front endpaper, 19, 48, 91, 104, 165, 166br, 167bl, 173

Zandra Rhodes Enterprises: /Patrick Anderson: 6tl; /Clive Arrowsmith: 6b; / Robyn Beeche: 6tr, 7, 153

Every effort has been made to acknowledge correctly and contact the source and/or copyright holder of each picture, and Carlton Books Limited apologizes for any unintentional errors or omissions, which will be corrected in future editions of this book.

Authors' Acknowledgments

Emma Baxter-Wright: Special thanks to Lisa Dyer for commissioning me. Dedicated to Dex, O, and Dusty Rose. **Karen Clarkson:** Dedicated to Nisse Sauerland, Simon Swift, and Hector, with love. **Sarah Kennedy:** Thanks to Lisa Helmanis, Emma Hodges, Carol McKeown, and Jane W. Kellock for fashion memories and positive inspiration. Dedicated to Duncan, Freddie, and Findlay, with love. **Kate Mulvey:** Dedicated to Georgia, Myles, George, and Oscar, with love.

Publisher's Acknowledgments

The publishers would especially like to thank Cleo and Mark Butterfield for their hospitality, warmth, and enthusiasm during the photography process, and particularly for their vast knowledge and expertise in helping to select from their amazing fashion archives. Thanks also go to Zandra Rhodes, for her rare artistry and fervent dedication to fashion heritage. Thanks to Bang Bang Clothing Exchange, 21 Goodge Street, London W1T 2PJ for the images of their shop on pages 208l, 208r, 209l, 211c, and 211r, taken by Emma Wright.